UnHUMAN

Dominick Clayton

UNHUMAN

Author
Dominick Clayton

Published by
One-L Group

Managing Editor
L. J. Petros

ISBN: 978-1-962250-20-7

Cover Design and Layout by
Jasmine C. Cole

UnHuman Chapter Breakdown

Dedication

To my beloved daughter, whose bright spirit and endless curiosity inspired me to write this book and leave a legacy. May you always chase our dreams with the same unwavering passion.

Foreword

by Adolphus Nolan, Advisor BH365 Education

To confront history is an act of courage. To challenge the narratives we've inherited, to bring light to truths that have been buried, and to refuse to let them be erased—that is a responsibility we must carry with conviction.

Dominick Clayton, my cousin and close friend for the past decade, has taken up this charge with the heart of an educator, the mind of a scholar, and the soul of a storyteller. *UnHuman: Why Has America Not Healed?* is not just a book; it is an invitation—an urgent call to examine the deeply ingrained wounds of our nation, to acknowledge the truths of our past, and to ask ourselves what it means to be fully human in the pursuit of justice and reconciliation.

For generations, history has been written by those in power, often at the expense of those whose stories were deemed inconvenient. To speak honestly about the past is not to wallow in grievance, but to reclaim agency over the narrative. Dominick understands that preserving and proliferating Black history is not just about documentation—it is about empowerment, about ensuring that we, and the generations that follow, stand on the firm ground of truth rather than the shifting sands of revisionism.

In the America we know today, where the highest offices seek to remove factually accurate curriculum from schools and where entire historical truths are being pulled from bookshelves, the act of telling the truth becomes revolutionary—and shouldn't be. It is a necessary rejection of erasure. As I reflect on Dominick's work in schools, social settings & stages, I am reminded that history is not a weapon to be wielded selectively; it is a mirror in which we must see ourselves fully—flaws, failures, and all.

Dominick has always been a relentless seeker of truth, a mentor in the classroom, and a father whose lessons extend well beyond his own upbringing. He has never shied away from difficult conversations - and ours are usually difficult - because he understands that avoidance does not absolve us. If we do not confront our history, we become complicit in its repetition. We must do more than simply pull the knife out; we must tend the wound, understand the depth of its impact, and commit to healing in full measure. More than a third of this read is an invitation to heal.

In *UnHuman*, Domnick challenges us to consider what it truly means to be... human. And if humanity is the ability to empathize, to learn, and to strive toward something better, then we must measure ourselves not by our intentions, but by our willingness to reckon with reality. No one is asking for a pound of flesh. No one is demanding a penance. But the past is not behind us; it is woven into the fabric of our present. It is up to us whether we use that fabric to build or to blindfold.

The words in the pages to follow will unsettle you. They will provoke, question, and demand engagement. And that is precisely why they must be read. Because the only way forward—the only truly human thing to do next—is to tell the truth.

QUESTION:

Why has America not healed?

ANSWER:

Dehumanization.

CHAPTER 1

Dehumanization

"History, despite its wrenching pain, cannot be unlived, but if faced with courage, need not be lived again." - Maya Angelou

What is my history? Where do I come from? Who do I come from? Who am I? These are questions many people can answer; however, these are questions many Black people in America simply cannot answer. Why? That is precisely my why. Why do I not know my family lineage past my great grandparents? And I barely know anything about them mind you. Where were my family's beginnings? That search has led me down the path of researching America's history. What I have found is that my existence as a Black man in America has not been valued, yet had a value placed on me and my fellow Black people as a commodity. America has not healed from its traumatic history because she has not addressed its most basic folly; the dehumanization of the people in America through the practice of enslaving humans.

Dehumanization is the process of depriving a person or group of positive human qualities. Malcolm X was asked, "Do you hate all white people?" His response describes the dehumanization of a race of people and their fight to simply learn to love themselves again:

"I don't think it's a fair question… the white man doesn't even come into my attitude. He, Mr. Muhammad teaches us to love our own kind and let the white man take care of himself. For a white man today sir after kidnapping millions of black people from Africa stripping them of all human characteristics and relegating them to the role of chattel or cattle or animals commodity merchandise that could be bought and sold at will and then a hundred years since the Emancipation Proclamation using every type of deceptive method to further us into slavery called second-class citizenship; I think that it would take a whole lot of nerve for white people today to ask Negroes do they hate them."

Malcolm X was talking about one form of dehumanization. We are going to explore many forms of dehumanization that has occurred in American history. See, the dehumanization that Malcolm X was referring to was that of those that were enslaved in America that were taken from Africa. Because of their dehumanization, they were denied many positive human rights. However, there were also those that were already here, the indigenous people, the people whose land was taken, the people whose freedom was taken, the people who were lumped into a category not even known by or represented by their known names at the time but called African Americans so that they could be all be lumped together. Another dehumanization tactic. There's also another form of dehumanization, those that enslaved people, those that stole the land, those that demoralized other human beings to build their generational wealth. It takes a certain mindset and perpetuation of that mindset to continually be able to see humans as unhuman. That mindset must be passed down from generation to generation and the result is unfortunately a dehumanized mind. That is a very dangerous mind. There's another type of dehumanization that's at play in America and those are the capitalistic ideals and businesses that have profited from the enslavement or dehumanization of others that constantly denied that they had a part in it. Yet, they profited from it. To continue that path of profit, as a nation and within a system of capitalism, one must dehumanize their mind and justify their actions by saying it wasn't me.

My Story:

When I was growing up in Orlando, Florida in the early 80's, my parents and family said to us that "we don't go to Ocoee, it's not safe for us there." As a child, that statement made no sense whatsoever to me. Why can we not go to Ocoee? Why is it not safe for 'us'? Who is 'us' anyway? Is just my family not safe to go there? Ocoee, Florida is a small suburb on the west side of Orlando, Florida. Well, when I was around four years old, I got my initial answer. My dad's new pit-bull puppy had just been stolen and my dad had a lead on where to find him. That lead led us to drive through Ocoee. I jumped in the car with him as he took off. I'll never forget because I never passed up the opportunity to ride in his candy apple red Monte Carlo! I was in the front seat that day and had my eyes glued to all my surroundings as we drove down highway 50, to the locals west colonial drive. I remember seeing two signs on the side of the road as we entered Ocoee. One read: "Welcome to Ocoee" while the other read "When the sun goes down, niggers better not be around." I immediately had a rush of fear run through my body from head to toe. I turned and asked my dad if we should drive through Ocoee. It was at that moment that I understood that it was not safe for Black people to be in Ocoee. But, why? How was this even still a thing in the 80's? How was this even legal? What happened?

Ocoee Massacre of 1920:

The Ocoee Massacre of 1920 was a violent incident that occurred in Ocoee, Florida, a small town just outside of Orlando. The massacre began on Election Day, November 2, 1920, when a Black man named July Perry attempted to vote. He was turned away from the polls and subsequently attacked by a group of white men. This incident sparked a wave of violence against Black citizens throughout the area.

White mobs attacked Black neighborhoods, burning homes and businesses, and forcing all of the Black families to flee for their lives. The violence resulted in the deaths of at least six Black people, although the exact number is unknown and still up for debate. Many more were injured, and countless others lost their homes and possessions.

The Ocoee Massacre was a clear example of how white supremacy and racism were deeply ingrained in American society, and how they could manifest in violent and deadly ways. The massacre also had long-lasting effects on the Black citizens of Orlando, who were further dehumanized by the violent actions of their white neighbors.

In the aftermath of the massacre, all the Black families were forced to leave the area, leaving behind their homes, businesses, and community. According to U.S. census data, no Black citizens lived in Ocoee from the time of massacre until around 1980. The Black homes and land that were left behind were then sold; however, the new deeds only allowed for the homes and land to be sold to White people. The fear and trauma of the violence continued to impact the Black community for decades to come, creating a legacy of racial inequality, loss of generational wealth and injustice.

The Ocoee Massacre serves as a reminder of the systemic racism that has persisted in America for centuries, and the devastating effects it has had on Black communities. It is important to acknowledge the atrocities of the past and work towards creating a more just and equitable society for all.

With dehumanization comes fear, denial, superiority complexes, and self-hate. All of these things combined make up dehumanization and what has happened in America for it not to heal. I'm interested in what America can do to heal. What we can do is face the fact that we have a history that is beautiful; that is ugly; that is positive; that is negative; that is forward looking, but also yet still preserves some of the very negative practices and mindsets that got us to where we are today.

I'm interested in what America can do to heal. The first step is to realize that we have dehumanized ourselves to the point where some of us are unhuman. We look at reality through a negatively skewed lens. We see each other as combatants or commodities, not human beings, not my fellow man. Not my American brother or sister. In this book, we are going to examine the ways in which we got here and the ways in which we can heal and move forward from here. I am truly interested in and dedicated to America healing and living up to her declaration as one nation, under God, indivisible, with liberty and justice for all.

CHAPTER 2
How We Got Here:
Slavery in America

Enslaved Africans in America:

The origins of slavery in America can be traced back to the early colonial period in the 17th century. At that time, European colonizers who settled in North America needed labor to cultivate crops, primarily tobacco, rice, and indigo. Initially, these colonizers relied on indentured servants, who were mostly poor Europeans who agreed to work for a set number of years in exchange for passage to the colonies. However, the supply of indentured servants started to dwindle, and as the demand for labor increased, plantation owners turned to enslaved Africans.

One of the primary reasons for the use of African slaves was their perceived economic value. At the time, Africa was a source of cheap labor, and the transatlantic slave trade provided a steady supply of enslaved Africans to the Americas. The practice of enslavement allowed plantation owners to acquire a large labor force at a relatively low cost, which in turn led to increased profits. Additionally, because slaves were considered property, plantation owners had a financial incentive to maximize their output and minimize costs, which often meant harsh and inhumane treatment of slaves.

Another reason for the use of slavery was the belief in white supremacy and racial hierarchy. European colonizers viewed themselves as superior to Africans and other non-white races, and the use of slavery helped reinforce their perceived superiority. The dehumanization of Africans was used to justify their enslavement and mistreatment, as it was believed that they were inherently inferior and unsuited for anything other than hard labor. This mindset was further entrenched by the development of racialized slavery laws and practices, which created a legal framework for the exploitation and oppression of Black people in America.

The Christian Black Codes of 1620 and Their Contribution to the Dehumanization of Blacks in America

The Christian Black Codes of 1620 were a set of legal and social codes implemented by European settlers in colonial America to govern the status of Black enslaved individuals. Though there were many variations of these codes throughout different colonies, their core principles revolved around control, dehumanization, and maintaining a racial caste system. While many specific details about the 1620 Christian Black Codes have been lost or evolved over time, the early colonial laws of the 17th century were a precursor to later codified racial segregation and dehumanization practices, such as the Black Codes in the 1800s.

Religious Justification for Dehumanization

The Christian Black Codes, which were rooted in a misguided interpretation of Christianity, played a crucial role in the process of dehumanizing enslaved Black people. Colonial powers framed enslavement as not only an economic necessity but also a moral and religious imperative. By misusing biblical scriptures, enslavers justified the enslavement of Africans as an act of divine will, claiming that they were "saving" Black people by bringing them into Christian civilization.

These codes worked in tandem with broader societal norms, laws, and customs that stripped Black people of their rights, their humanity, and their status as individuals. Enslaved Africans were legally defined as property rather than people, paving the way for centuries of violence, discrimination, and exploitation.

Dehumanization Through Legal Restrictions

The Christian Black Codes denied Black individuals the right to basic human freedoms, reinforcing a system of subjugation. Key elements of these codes included:

1. **Religious Hierarchy:** The Codes required that enslaved Africans adopt Christianity, but paradoxically, conversion did not grant them freedom or equal treatment. Instead, it reinforced the idea that their enslaved status was divinely ordained. This form of religious manipulation was used to pacify resistance and justify continued enslavement.

2. **Marriage and Family Restrictions:** The Codes prevented enslaved people from legally marrying, which effectively undermined family structures. The separation of enslaved families was common, as enslaved people could be sold or traded at will, with no legal recourse to maintain their family units.

3. **Forbidding Education:** Black people were barred from receiving an education under these codes, which contributed to their dehumanization by keeping them in a state of enforced ignorance. Prohibiting literacy ensured that enslaved individuals were unable to communicate effectively, organize, or develop the intellectual tools needed to challenge their subjugation.

4. **Physical Violence and Punishment:** The Codes authorized extreme physical punishment and violence to control enslaved populations. Whippings, mutilations, and executions were legal forms of discipline, used to maintain a climate of fear and total obedience.

5. **Enslavement Based on Race:** The Christian Black Codes established a racial hierarchy, with Black people relegated to the lowest social and economic status. Enslavement became based on skin color, thus embedding racism into the legal fabric of American society.

Lasting Impact of the Christian Black Codes

The Christian Black Codes laid the foundation for a system that systematically dehumanized Black people for centuries. They contributed to the development of more formalized and extensive legal structures, such as the Slave Codes, Jim Crow laws, and other forms of institutionalized racism that persisted well into the 20th century and beyond.

This legal dehumanization created a culture that viewed Black people as inferior and reinforced a societal framework in which their lives were devalued. Even after the formal abolition of slavery, the social and psychological effects of these laws continued to influence racial discrimination in America, manifesting in structural inequality, police violence, and mass incarceration.

The Christian Black Codes of 1620 were an early and critical part of America's legacy of dehumanization and racial oppression. By legally codifying the inferiority of Black people and denying them basic human rights, these laws perpetuated a culture of racial hierarchy that justified centuries of violence and subjugation. The legacy of these codes can still be felt today, as the structural and institutional remnants of this dehumanization continue to impact Black communities in the U.S.

The Story of Olaudah Equiano

Olaudah Equiano was a prominent African writer and abolitionist who was enslaved in America. Born in what is now Nigeria, he was kidnapped and sold into slavery at the age of 11. Equiano was transported to America where he was sold to various slave masters and forced to work on plantations in the Southern states.

Equiano was one of the few enslaved Africans who learned to read and write, and he used this skill to document his experiences and advocate for the abolition of slavery. In his autobiography, "The Interesting Narrative of the Life of Olaudah Equiano," he vividly described the brutalities he and other enslaved Africans endured, including beatings, torture, and separation from their families.

Equiano's experiences and writings led him to become an influential advocate for the abolition of slavery. In 1789, he wrote a letter to the Queen of England in which he passionately pleaded for an end to the transatlantic slave trade. In the letter, he argued that the slave trade was morally wrong and that it was economically unsustainable, as it depended on the exploitation of African labor.

Equiano also used his platform to petition the British government to abolish slavery in its colonies, including America. He traveled extensively throughout Europe, giving lectures and speeches about the horrors of slavery and the need for abolition. His advocacy was instrumental in the eventual passage of the British Slave Trade Act of 1807, which abolished the transatlantic slave trade.

Equiano's writings and advocacy played a significant role in the movement to abolish slavery in America and beyond. His life story stands as a testament to the resilience and perseverance of enslaved Africans, and his legacy continues to inspire efforts to promote justice and equality around the world.

The use of slavery as an economic model in America was driven by the demand for labor, the availability of cheap African labor through the transatlantic slave trade, and the belief in white supremacy and racial hierarchy. These factors combined to create a system of institutionalized racism and oppression that has had lasting effects on American society and continues to be felt today.

Native Americans and Slavery in America:

The history of America enslaving Native Americans is a tragic and often overlooked aspect of American history. The enslavement of Native Americans began with the arrival of European colonizers in the Americas in the 15th and 16th centuries. From the very beginning, European colonizers saw Native Americans as inferior and exploitable, and they began to enslave them to build their colonies and extract resources from the land.

One of the earliest instances of Native American enslavement was during the Spanish conquest of the Americas. The Spanish brought African slaves with them to the Americas, but they also enslaved Native Americans, particularly the Arawak people of the Caribbean. The Arawaks were forced to work in gold mines and on plantations, and their population was decimated by the brutal conditions of their enslavement.

Christopher Columbus is often mythologized as the bold explorer who "discovered" the Americas in 1492, but the reality of his interactions with the indigenous peoples he encountered is far darker. His arrival in the Caribbean marked the beginning of a violent era of conquest, colonization, and systemic dehumanization that would forever alter the lives of Native Americans. Columbus' expeditions set the stage for centuries of exploitation and cruelty, with the indigenous peoples suffering the brunt of this inhumanity.

When Columbus first arrived in what is now the Bahamas, he encountered the Taíno people. His initial impressions, recorded in his logbook, highlight a dichotomy that would characterize European interactions with indigenous populations for centuries to come. On one hand, Columbus noted the natives' generosity, peaceful nature, and willingness to share. In his first description of the Taíno, he marveled at their hospitality, writing:

"They are very gentle and without knowledge of what is evil; nor do they murder or steal... Your Highness may believe that in all the world there can be no better people."

However, within the same observations, Columbus began to view the Taíno not as fellow human beings, but as resources to be exploited. In the same log entry, he remarked:

"With fifty men, they could all be subjugated and made to do what is required of them."

From the outset, Columbus viewed the native populations as people to be dominated, commodified, and controlled. Despite recognizing their humanity, he quickly dehumanized them, reducing them to tools for imperial and economic gain.

Enslavement and Forced Labor

The dehumanization of the natives became clear as Columbus' expeditions continued. By the time of his second voyage in 1493, he had already begun implementing systems of forced labor. Columbus and his men enslaved many of the Taíno people and shipped them back to Spain to be sold. Those who remained were forced to work in brutal conditions, mining for gold or working on plantations established by the Spanish.

The encomienda system, introduced by Columbus, formalized this forced labor. It allowed the Spanish settlers to "entrust" a group of indigenous people to a colonist, who in turn was supposed to protect them and teach them Christianity. In practice, it was slavery in all but name. The indigenous people were forced to work under threat of violence, and many died from overwork, malnutrition, or disease brought by the Europeans.

Columbus rationalized his exploitation of the indigenous people by viewing them as lesser beings, capable only of serving the needs of their European "superiors." This mindset of inherent superiority enabled the violence and degradation that the indigenous people suffered at the hands of the Spanish colonists.

Systemic Violence and Brutality

As Columbus and his men expanded their presence in the Caribbean, violence became an ever-present tool of control. The initial awe and wonder he expressed in his early letters turned into outright disdain and cruelty when the native populations resisted Spanish demands. Columbus and his men resorted to extreme forms of violence to subjugate the Taíno, including mutilation, murder, and mass executions.

One particularly brutal practice was the cutting off of hands. Natives who failed to meet the impossible gold quotas imposed by Columbus' regime had their hands cut off as punishment. Many bled to death from these injuries. Columbus also engaged in mass punishment, executing entire groups of indigenous people to send a message of fear and submission.

Moreover, women and girls were subjected to sexual violence by Columbus' men, who raped and exploited them with impunity. Columbus himself wrote about gifting women to his men as rewards for their loyalty. The sexual abuse of indigenous women became another form of dehumanization, reducing them to objects of desire to be traded and used by the Spanish colonizers.

The Decimation of the Native Population

The arrival of Columbus and his men had catastrophic consequences for the indigenous populations of the Caribbean. While violence and forced labor were primary causes of death, European diseases such as smallpox, measles, and influenza devastated the native peoples, who had no immunity to these foreign illnesses.

In just a few decades, the Taíno population of Hispaniola (modern-day Haiti and the Dominican Republic), where Columbus first established a colony, fell from an estimated one million people to a few thousand. Entire communities were wiped out, and the social fabric of the indigenous peoples was shattered.

The depopulation of the Caribbean was not seen as a tragedy by Columbus and the Spanish, but as an unfortunate byproduct of their quest for wealth and glory. The indigenous people, having been dehumanized by Columbus and other colonizers, were seen as expendable in the pursuit of gold and territory.

Religious Justification for Dehumanization

One of the most insidious aspects of Columbus' dehumanization of indigenous peoples was his use of religion to justify his actions. Columbus saw himself as a crusader for Christianity, and he viewed the forced conversion of the indigenous people as part of his divine mission. He described his expeditions in religious terms, claiming that his goal was to bring the light of Christianity to the "savages" of the New World.

However, this religious mission was a pretext for conquest and domination. The indigenous peoples were not treated as spiritual equals but as souls to be converted by force. Those who resisted were considered enemies of Christianity and were subjected to brutal punishment. The forced baptisms of the indigenous people were hollow, as they continued to be enslaved and oppressed even after their conversion. This blending of religious justification and colonial violence created a framework in which dehumanization was both morally sanctioned and legally enforced.

Legacy of Dehumanization

Columbus' dehumanizing treatment of the indigenous peoples he encountered had far-reaching consequences. His actions set the precedent for future European colonization of the Americas, where indigenous populations were routinely enslaved, exterminated, or displaced in the pursuit of land and wealth. The pattern of dehumanization established by Columbus—viewing native peoples as lesser beings to be dominated and exploited—became a central tenet of European colonialism in the New World.

Columbus' legacy, often celebrated in history textbooks as one of exploration and discovery, is far more complex and troubling. While he undeniably altered the course of world history, his voyages also initiated a centuries-long period of violence and dehumanization against indigenous peoples that continues to reverberate to this day.

Christopher Columbus' expeditions to the Americas marked the beginning of a devastating era for the native populations of the Caribbean and the broader Americas. His initial encounters with the Taíno people demonstrated a brief recognition of their humanity, but his actions quickly shifted to dehumanization, enslavement, and violence. By viewing indigenous peoples as resources to be exploited and using religion as a justification for their oppression, Columbus established a model of dehumanization that would be followed by European powers for centuries.

The dehumanization of native peoples laid the groundwork for the systemic inequalities and racial hierarchies that persist in the Americas today. To truly understand Columbus' legacy, we must confront the dark reality of how his voyages contributed to the suffering and marginalization of millions of indigenous people. Only by acknowledging this history can we begin to address the lasting impact of these injustices and work toward a more equitable and just future for all people.

In the British colonies, Native Americans were also enslaved, particularly in the southern colonies. Enslavement of Native Americans was often used as a way to punish tribes that resisted colonization, and it was also used to acquire land. The British passed laws that allowed them to enslave Native Americans who were taken as prisoners of war, and Native American slaves were used to work on plantations and in other industries.

The French also enslaved Native Americans in their colonies, particularly in Canada. The French saw Native Americans as "savages" who needed to be "civilized" and converted to Christianity, and they used enslavement to force their cultural and religious beliefs on the Native population.

The reasons behind the enslavement of Native Americans were varied, but they all stemmed from a belief in the superiority of European culture and the idea that Native Americans were "uncivilized" and in need of "civilizing." Enslavement was also seen as a strategy to acquire land and resources, and as a punishment for tribes that resisted colonization.

Today, the enslavement of Native Americans is a largely forgotten part of American history, but it had a profound impact on Native populations and contributed to the ongoing marginalization and oppression of Native peoples. Understanding this history is crucial to addressing the systemic issues that continue to affect Native communities today.

The Raw History of Thanksgiving

Thanksgiving is a holiday celebrated annually in the United States on the fourth Thursday in November. It is a day where people gather with their families and loved ones to express gratitude and share a meal. The holiday has a controversial history, particularly regarding its origins and the treatment of Native Americans.

Many people believe that the first Thanksgiving was a peaceful gathering between the Pilgrims and the Wampanoag tribe in 1621. However, this narrative ignores the violence and oppression that the Pilgrims and other European settlers inflicted upon the Native American peoples.

The colonization of America by Europeans led to the displacement and genocide of countless Native Americans. The first encounters between Europeans and Native Americans were often violent, with Europeans seizing Native American lands and resources.

The Wampanoag tribe, who are often portrayed as peaceful hosts at the first Thanksgiving, were actually forced to sign a treaty with the Pilgrims in 1621, which essentially surrendered their lands to the European settlers. The treaty was not a peaceful agreement, but rather a result of the Wampanoag being weakened by diseases brought by the Europeans, such as smallpox.

Furthermore, the Pilgrims did not celebrate Thanksgiving annually, but rather held sporadic feasts to give thanks for bountiful harvests or military victories. The holiday did not become an annual tradition until the mid-19th century, during a time when relations between Native Americans and European settlers were at their worst.

In recent years, there has been a push to acknowledge the true history of Thanksgiving and to recognize the suffering and injustices inflicted upon Native American peoples. Some Native American communities have started to observe the holiday as a National Day of Mourning, to honor the lives lost and to call for justice and reconciliation.

It is important to acknowledge and learn from the past in order to create a more just and equitable future for all peoples. The dehumanization of enslaved Africans and enslaved natives in America had a profound and lasting impact on both groups. Enslaved Africans were forcibly taken from their homelands, stripped of their identities, and reduced to property. They were subjected to brutal and inhumane treatment, including physical abuse, forced labor, and sexual exploitation. This dehumanization led to a lasting legacy of systemic racism and oppression that continues to affect Black Americans to this day.

Similarly, Native Americans were subjected to a centuries-long campaign of violence, displacement, and cultural erasure. Their land was stolen, their families were forcibly removed from their homes and sent to live on reservations, and their traditions and languages were suppressed. The dehumanization of Native Americans had a devastating impact on their communities, leading to intergenerational trauma, poverty, and marginalization.

Both groups have experienced ongoing discrimination and inequality because of the dehumanization they faced in America. The legacy of slavery and Native American genocide continues to shape the social and political landscape of America, and addressing these historical injustices remains a crucial step in achieving true equality, justice for all, and healing for ALL Americans.

CHAPTER 3:
Systems of Oppression
American Laws that Dehumanized enslaved people and their impact today

Throughout American history, there were numerous laws that were designed to dehumanize and control enslaved people. These laws often treated enslaved people as property rather than as human beings and stripped them of their basic rights and freedoms.

One of the earliest laws that dehumanized enslaved people was the Virginia Slave Code of 1705, which defined enslaved people as "chattel" or property. This law denied enslaved people the right to own property, marry, or assemble without permission. It also made it a crime to teach enslaved people to read or write, as education was seen as a threat to the system of slavery.

The Fugitive Slave Act of 1850 was another law that dehumanized enslaved people. This law required all citizens to assist in the capture and return of runaway enslaved people, regardless of their own beliefs or values. The law also denied enslaved people the right to a trial by jury and made it illegal for anyone to help them escape to freedom.

The Dred Scott v. Sandford decision of 1857 was a Supreme Court case that further dehumanized enslaved people. The Court ruled that enslaved people were not citizens and had no rights under the Constitution, which meant that they could not sue in federal court or seek protection from the law. This decision strengthened the institution of slavery and helped to push the country towards the Civil War.

In addition to these laws, there were also many local and state regulations that dehumanized enslaved people. For example, in Louisiana, enslaved people were required to carry passes whenever they left their owner's property. In South Carolina, enslaved people could be punished with branding or dismemberment for crimes such as running away or stealing.

Overall, these laws and regulations were designed to maintain the dehumanizing system of slavery, and they had an overwhelming impact on the lives of enslaved people. It was not until the end of the Civil War and the passage of the 13th, 14th, and 15th Amendments to the Constitution that enslaved people were legally recognized as citizens with basic rights and freedoms.

Compromise of 1877 leads to Jim Crow Laws:

The Compromise of 1877 was an informal agreement between Southern Democrats and Northern Republicans that marked the end of Reconstruction in the United States. As part of the compromise, Southern Democrats agreed to support Republican Rutherford B. Hayes' bid for the presidency in exchange for the removal of federal troops from the South, effectively ending federal intervention in Southern politics and paving the way for the establishment of Jim Crow laws.

Jim Crow laws were a series of state and local laws in the United States that enforced racial segregation and discrimination against black people from the late 19th century to the mid-1960s. These laws, which were prevalent in the Southern United States, mandated segregation in public spaces such as schools, transportation, and housing, and denied Black people the right to vote through various means, including poll taxes, literacy tests, and violence. Here are some specific examples of Jim Crow Laws that dehumanized Black people in America:

1. **Segregated Schools:** Jim Crow Laws enforced racial segregation in schools, with Black children attending separate, underfunded and often inferior schools. The Supreme Court case Plessy v. Ferguson (1896) upheld the constitutionality of "separate but equal" facilities, allowing for segregation in public schools and other public places.

2. **Poll Taxes and Literacy Tests:** Jim Crow Laws often required Black voters to pay a poll tax or take a literacy test in order to vote. These requirements were designed to prevent Black Americans from participating in the political process, and to preserve the power of White politicians.

3. **Separate Drinking Fountains and Restrooms:** Jim Crow Laws mandated separate drinking fountains, restrooms, and other public facilities for Black and White people. These facilities were often of inferior quality for Black people and were designed to reinforce the idea that Black people were inferior to white people.

4. **Discrimination in Housing:** Jim Crow Laws allowed for discrimination in housing, making it difficult for Black people to buy or rent homes in certain neighborhoods. This led to the creation of ghettos and other segregated neighborhoods where Black people were forced to live.

5. **Anti-Miscegenation Laws:** Jim Crow Laws also prohibited interracial marriage, making it illegal for Black people to marry White people. This was designed to prevent the mixing of races and to reinforce the idea of white supremacy.

These examples show how Jim Crow Laws dehumanized Black people in America, denying them basic civil rights and enforcing a system of racial segregation and discrimination.

The Compromise of 1877 played a significant role in the establishment of Jim Crow laws by creating a power vacuum in the South that allowed white supremacist groups to gain political control and push for segregationist policies. In many cases, these policies were enforced through violence, intimidation, and the threat of economic retribution, which further dehumanized Black people and reinforced white supremacy.

The Jim Crow era had a lasting impact on American society, as it perpetuated racial inequality and segregation, denied black people access to basic civil rights and liberties, and created a legacy of systemic racism that continues to shape the United States today. While significant progress has been made in the fight for racial equality, the legacy of Jim Crow remains an important reminder of the ongoing struggle for social justice and the need for continued efforts to dismantle systems of oppression and discrimination.

The 13th Amendment and the Continuation of Slavery in a New Form

The 13th Amendment to the U.S. Constitution, ratified in 1865, is often celebrated as the amendment that abolished slavery in the United States. Its first section explicitly states:

"Neither slavery nor involuntary servitude, except as a punishment for crime whereof the party shall have been duly convicted, shall exist within the United States, or any place subject to their jurisdiction."

While the 13th Amendment is credited with formally ending slavery, the inclusion of the phrase "except as a punishment for crime" created a loophole that allowed slavery to continue in another form—through the criminal justice system. This clause permitted the enslavement of individuals convicted of a crime, leading to the widespread use of convict labor, particularly targeting Black Americans in the aftermath of the Civil War.

Convict Leasing: A New Form of Slavery

In the decades following the Civil War, southern states, devastated by the loss of free labor from enslaved people, found a way to maintain racial control and rebuild their economy through the system of convict leasing. This practice allowed private companies and individuals to "lease" prisoners from state governments to work in mines, plantations, railroads, and factories, often in conditions that were just as brutal as slavery. Convicts, overwhelmingly Black and arrested for minor offenses such as vagrancy or loitering, were subjected to grueling labor, physical abuse, and inhumane living conditions.

Many states passed Black Codes, laws designed to criminalize minor actions for Black people, including loitering, unemployment, or breaking curfew. These laws disproportionately targeted freed Black Americans, leading to mass incarcerations and feeding a steady supply of free labor back to the very industries that had thrived on slavery.

The Prison Industrial Complex

Even after the official end of convict leasing in the early 20th century, the use of prison labor persisted. Today, the prison-industrial complex continues to profit from the labor of incarcerated people. Many private companies use prison labor to manufacture goods, from textiles to electronics, paying prisoners pennies on the dollar for their work. These individuals, most of whom are people of color, particularly Black Americans, are subjected to exploitation, unable to refuse work under threat of punishment.

The over-policing and mass incarceration of Black and brown communities, a legacy of the 13th Amendment's loophole, has led to disproportionately high imprisonment rates among these populations, further perpetuating a system of racial inequality. Today, the U.S. holds about 5% of the world's population but nearly 25% of the world's incarcerated people, with Black men incarcerated at five times the rate of white men. The persistence of racial disparities in the criminal justice system reflects the lingering effects of this amendment's exception clause.

Modern-Day Implications

The 13th Amendment's loophole continues to impact millions of lives. Mass incarceration and prison labor have become modern iterations of the racialized control mechanisms once formalized through slavery. The dehumanization of incarcerated individuals, especially those from marginalized communities, echoes the exploitation of enslaved people in the antebellum South.

Activists and scholars, such as Michelle Alexander, author of The New Jim Crow, argue that the current system of mass incarceration is an extension of racial control that began with slavery, persisted through Jim Crow, and continues today. The fight for true freedom and equality for Black Americans, therefore, remains incomplete as long as the 13th Amendment's exception clause remains in place, allowing for the exploitation of incarcerated individuals as a new form of slavery.

While the 13th Amendment officially abolished slavery, it also created a legal loophole that allowed slavery to continue under the guise of punishment for crime. This loophole has led to the perpetuation of racial control and exploitation through the criminal justice system, a legacy that continues to shape American society today.

Federal Laws that Dehumanized Black Americans

There have been various federal laws throughout American history that have dehumanized Black Americans, both in the past and present. Here are some examples:

1. **Fugitive Slave Act of 1850:** This law required the return of escaped slaves to their owners, regardless of whether they had made it to a free state or not. It essentially treated enslaved people as property rather than human beings with agency.

2. **Plessy v. Ferguson (1896):** This Supreme Court decision established the "separate but equal" doctrine, which allowed for racial segregation in public facilities. This law essentially codified racial discrimination and further dehumanized Black Americans by treating them as inferior and unworthy of equal treatment.

3. **Redlining (1930s-1960s):** This was a federal policy that prevented Black Americans from obtaining mortgages or other loans to purchase homes in certain neighborhoods. This resulted in the segregation of neighborhoods and the concentration of poverty in Black communities, further dehumanizing Black Americans by limiting their access to economic opportunities and perpetuating cycles of poverty.

4. **War on Drugs (1970s-1990s):** This federal policy, which was ostensibly aimed at reducing drug use and trafficking, disproportionately targeted Black Americans and resulted in the mass incarceration of Black people. The harsh sentencing guidelines and mandatory minimums for drug offenses resulted in a significant number of Black people being locked up

for nonviolent offenses, further dehumanizing them by treating them as criminals and perpetuating the stereotype of Black people as inherently criminal.

5. **Voter suppression laws:** In recent years, there have been numerous laws passed at the state and federal levels that make it harder for Black Americans to vote, including strict voter ID laws, limiting early voting, and closing polling locations in predominantly Black neighborhoods. These laws serve to dehumanize Black Americans by denying them the right to participate in the democratic process and perpetuating the idea that their voices and votes do not matter.

Dehumanizing treatment of Black Soldiers in America

Black soldiers who served in World War I faced dehumanizing treatment upon their return home to the United States. Despite their sacrifice and service to their country, they were still viewed as inferior and treated as second-class citizens. Black soldiers faced discrimination and violence before, during, and after the war, including segregation within the military, unequal pay, and being denied access to benefits and services provided to White soldiers.

After the war, many Black soldiers were also subject to violence and lynchings, especially in the South. The violence was often carried out by White mobs who resented the gains made by Black soldiers during the war, including increased access to education, jobs, and voting rights. In some cases, Black soldiers were targeted specifically because they had dared to wear their uniforms or display their military honors in public.

The Red Summer of 1919 was a period of intense racial violence and unrest that occurred across the United States, primarily in urban areas, during the summer and early fall of that year. The violence was largely directed against Black soldiers returning from World War I.

During the war, Black soldiers served with distinction and had been promised greater rights and opportunities upon their return, just like they were promised for fighting in the American Revolution and the Civil Way. However, many White Americans were deeply threatened by the prospect of Black soldiers claiming a greater stake in American society, and tensions began to rise as soldiers returned home.

In the summer of 1919, race riots broke out in cities across the country, including Chicago, Washington D.C., and Omaha, among others. Black communities were targeted by White mobs, who burned homes and businesses and attacked Black residents with guns, clubs, and other weapons.

Black soldiers returning from the war were often singled out for particularly brutal treatment. Many were attacked and lynched by White mobs, and some were even killed in uniform, with their military status providing no protection against the dehumanizing violence. Leaving many to wonder why they continue to love and fight for a country who clearly does not love nor fight for them.

The Red Summer of 1919 was a clear demonstration of the deep-seated racism and dehumanization that was present in American society at the time. The violence and injustice that Black soldiers and other African Americans experienced during this period served as a stark reminder that, despite their service and sacrifice, they were not seen as fully human in the eyes of many White Americans.

In addition to facing physical violence, Black soldiers were also subject to psychological abuse and mistreatment. Many were denied the opportunity to receive medical treatment, and some were even used as test subjects in unethical medical experiments. The dehumanizing treatment of Black soldiers after World War I further entrenched the systemic racism that already existed in the United States and created lasting detrimental impacts on Black communities that are still felt today.

Dehumanizing Medical Experiments on Black Americans:

Throughout American history, enslaved and Black people have been subjected to dehumanizing medical experiments without their consent or knowledge. This practice began during slavery, where enslaved people were seen as property rather than human beings with rights. Physicians and medical practitioners were able to conduct experiments on enslaved people with little to no consequences. These experiments included surgeries without anesthesia, forced blood transfusions, and the testing of various medicines and treatments. This practice continued long after slavery was "abolished."

One infamous case is the Tuskegee syphilis experiment, which began in 1932 and lasted for 40 years. The U.S. Public Health Service conducted this study on 600 Black men, 399 of whom had syphilis and 201 who did not. The study was supposed to observe the natural progression of untreated syphilis, but the participants were not told they had syphilis, nor were they treated for it. Even after penicillin was discovered as a cure for syphilis in the 1940s, the participants were still not given the treatment. As a result, many of them suffered severe health complications, including blindness, deafness, and death.

Another example is the case of J. Marion Sims, considered the father of modern gynecology. Sims performed numerous experimental surgeries on enslaved women in the mid-19th century, often without anesthesia or consent. He believed that Black women had a higher pain tolerance and could withstand the surgeries better than white women. This mindset still persists today within many healthcare professionals. Sims also conducted experiments on infants and children, often resulting in their death.

The Dehumanizing Medical Experiments on Henrietta Lacks

Henrietta Lacks, an African American woman, became an unwitting contributor to one of the most important breakthroughs in medical science, but her contribution came at the cost of her dignity, autonomy, and humanity. Born in 1920 in Roanoke, Virginia, Lacks sought treatment for cervical cancer at Johns Hopkins Hospital in 1951, one of the few medical institutions that treated Black patients during the era of racial segregation.

Without her knowledge or consent, doctors at Johns Hopkins took a sample of Lacks' cancerous cells during her treatment. Those cells, later known as HeLa cells, were found to have unique properties: they could survive and reproduce indefinitely in laboratory conditions. This made HeLa cells the first "immortal" human cell line, which has since been used in thousands of scientific studies and medical advancements, including the development of the polio vaccine, cancer research, gene mapping, and even treatments for AIDS.

Dehumanization Through Exploitation

Henrietta Lacks was never informed that her cells were taken, nor was her family made aware of their use until decades later. This lack of consent was emblematic of a broader pattern of medical exploitation and dehumanization of Black bodies, particularly of Black women, in American medical history. In Lacks' case, her body was treated as a resource, separate from her personhood, and the ethical considerations that should have been extended to her as a patient were ignored. Her treatment by the medical community reflected the legacy of slavery and systemic racism, in which Black individuals were often viewed as subjects for experimentation rather than as human beings deserving of dignity and agency.

Lacks and her family received no compensation for the use of her cells, even though her immortal HeLa cells revolutionized medicine and led to the generation of millions of dollars for pharmaceutical and research industries. Her identity was also initially concealed, with the cells referred to as coming from "Helen Lane" or other pseudonyms, further erasing her personal history and humanity.

Impact on Her Family

The medical community's exploitation of Lacks' cells caused ongoing trauma for her family. They were unaware of the cells' existence for more than two decades, and when they eventually learned the truth, they were thrust into the spotlight without adequate explanation, support, or compensation. The family's lack of understanding about how Henrietta's cells were being used—along with their exclusion from the medical and scientific discussions surrounding the HeLa cells—fueled feelings of betrayal, distrust, and dehumanization.

While medical researchers profited from the HeLa cells, Henrietta Lacks' family, like many African Americans, faced barriers to accessing basic healthcare. The stark contrast between the wealth generated by Henrietta's cells and the ongoing struggles of her family highlights the systemic inequalities that marginalized Black Americans in the healthcare system for generations.

Legacy and Change

In the years since the unethical treatment of Henrietta Lacks came to light, her story has sparked important discussions about medical ethics, consent, and the exploitation of marginalized communities. The story of HeLa cells prompted reforms to the ways research subjects are treated, and it led to demands for increased transparency and accountability in the field of biomedical research.

Henrietta Lacks' contribution to science cannot be overstated, but the dehumanizing way in which she and her family were treated underscores the long-standing racial injustices in medicine. Today, her story is recognized as a critical chapter in the struggle for medical justice and equity for Black Americans, and it serves as a reminder of the importance of ethical standards in research that respect the dignity and rights of all individuals.

Henrietta Lacks' legacy has been immortalized not just through her cells but also in efforts to improve patient rights, promote informed consent, and reckon with the racist history of medical experimentation in America.

These dehumanizing medical experiments had a long-lasting impact on Black communities, eroding trust in the medical system and contributing to healthcare disparities that still exist today. The legacy of these experiments underscores the ongoing need for ethical medical research and the importance of informed consent and respect for human dignity in medical practice.

Dehumanized Mindset of Capitalism – Americans & Businesses who profited from Slavery:

Throughout American history, businesses and people who did not own slaves still profited from slavery and participated in the dehumanization of Black Americans. The economy of the United States was built on the labor of enslaved people, and even after slavery was abolished, businesses continued to benefit from the exploitation of Black labor through sharecropping, segregation, convict leasing, and discriminatory hiring practices.

Many industries, such as the cotton and tobacco industries, were built on the backs of enslaved labor. Northern textile mills were also major beneficiaries of the slave trade, as they purchased the cotton produced by enslaved labor in the South. These industries and their owners profited immensely from slavery, and their wealth and success were built on the oppression and dehumanization of Black Americans.

Additionally, many businesses in the North and South continued to profit from the exploitation of Black labor after slavery was abolished. Sharecropping, a system in which Black farmers worked the land owned by White landowners and were paid a small share of the profits, was essentially a form of debt slavery that kept Black families trapped in poverty and prevented them from accumulating wealth.

Segregation also allowed businesses to exploit Black labor by paying Black workers less than White workers for the same work and denying Black workers access to education and job training programs. Discriminatory hiring practices and lack of access to capital have also made it more difficult for Black Americans to start their own businesses and accumulate wealth.

The effects of these dehumanizing practices are still felt today, as Black Americans continue to face systemic barriers to economic mobility and are disproportionately represented in low-paying, insecure jobs. Black families also continue to have significantly less wealth than White families, which is in part due to the historic and ongoing exploitation of Black labor.

To address these dehumanizing effects, businesses and individuals can take steps to acknowledge and repair the harm caused by historic and ongoing exploitation of Black labor. This can include supporting Black-owned businesses, investing in education and training programs that specifically target underrepresented groups, and advocating for policies that promote economic equality and dismantle systemic barriers to mobility. By actively working to promote economic justice and equity, individuals and businesses can begin to repair the dehumanization that has been caused by their participation in exploitative systems.

Businesses that profited from slavery:

There were many corporations and businesses that profited from slavery in America, and some of these companies still exist today. For example, the Lehman Brothers, one of the largest investment banks in the world, can trace its roots back to the 19th century when it was a cotton trading company that profited from slave labor in Alabama. Another example is Aetna, a major insurance company, which sold policies covering slaves and their owners, profiting from the exploitation of human beings.

J.P. Morgan Chase is another example of a company with a history of profiting from slavery. In the 1800s, the bank accepted enslaved people as collateral for loans, and in the early 20th century, it financed companies that used forced labor in the Congo. Wells Fargo also has a history of profiting from slavery, as it owned a number of slaves and lent money to slave owners.

Other companies that have been linked to the slave trade include New York Life, Tiffany & Co., and CSX Corporation. The impact of these companies' involvement in the slave trade is still felt today, as the wealth and power that these companies amassed through the exploitation of human beings have been passed down through generations, contributing to the systemic inequalities that still exist in our society.

It is important for these companies to acknowledge their history and take responsibility for the harm they caused. They can do so by supporting reparations for descendants of enslaved people, investing in communities that have been impacted by slavery and systemic racism, and ensuring that their current practices promote racial justice and equality.

CHAPTER 4
From Slavery to Civil Rights
Why the Fight for Civil Rights Is Not the Same as Human Rights in America

In the United States, the fight for civil rights has often been seen as synonymous with the broader struggle for human rights, but these are two distinct concepts with significant differences in scope, application, and intent. While civil rights refer to the rights guaranteed by a specific government—typically outlined in national law or the Constitution—human rights are universal, inherent to all individuals by virtue of being human and recognized globally by international declarations like the Universal Declaration of Human Rights (UDHR).

Civil Rights in America: Legal and National Context

Civil rights in America are rooted in the Constitution and its amendments, especially the Bill of Rights, and later reforms like the Civil Rights Act of 1964 and the Voting Rights Act of 1965. These laws aim to ensure equal treatment and protection under the law for all citizens, specifically targeting issues such as racial segregation, voting rights, and discrimination based on race, gender, religion, and more.

However, civil rights are rights granted by the state and can be limited, negotiated, or revoked by the same entity. For example, the Jim Crow laws of the 19th and 20th centuries enforced racial segregation, effectively stripping Black Americans of many civil rights guaranteed by the Constitution. Thus, the fight for civil rights is often framed as a battle for inclusion within the nation's legal framework, rather than the inherent rights of individuals as human beings.

Human Rights: A Broader, Universal Standard

Human rights, on the other hand, are universal and apply to all people regardless of nationality, race, or citizenship. They encompass not only civil and political rights, such as the right to vote or the right to free speech, but also social, economic, and cultural rights, such as the right to education, health care, and a living wage. These rights are not dependent on a government's recognition, and their violation is considered a breach of universal standards, as recognized by international bodies like the United Nations.

In the U.S., the fight for civil rights has traditionally focused on correcting domestic racial and social injustices, particularly against African Americans, but this has often been limited to seeking protections under U.S. law rather than aligning with the broader global framework of human rights. For example, many key elements of human rights—such as affordable healthcare, housing, and economic equality—are still not universally guaranteed in the U.S., despite their recognition as fundamental human rights by international standards.

The Limitations of Civil Rights vs. Human Rights

The civil rights movement of the 1950s and 1960s primarily fought for the end of legal segregation, the right to vote, and equal access to public spaces. These were all legal battles fought within the framework of U.S. law, seeking to ensure that Black Americans could enjoy the same rights that white Americans already had. However, this focus on legal equality under the Constitution did not necessarily address broader issues of systemic inequality, such as poverty, police brutality, or economic exploitation, which are more in line with human rights violations.

For instance, while civil rights laws may prohibit employment discrimination, they do not guarantee a living wage or access to healthcare, which are fundamental human rights under international standards. The U.S. often fails to recognize these as basic rights, limiting the scope of the fight for justice to narrower legal concerns rather than tackling the full spectrum of human needs.

The Fight for Human Rights in the U.S.: Ongoing Struggles

In many ways, the broader fight for human rights remains unfulfilled in the United States. Issues such as mass incarceration, police violence, economic inequality, and healthcare disparities disproportionately affect Black and Brown communities, revealing the limitations of focusing solely on civil rights. While legal victories have been won, many of the systemic conditions that prevent true equality and justice persist.

The fight for human rights requires addressing the structural inequalities that affect people's access to basic necessities and freedoms. The U.S. has often resisted incorporating international human rights frameworks into its domestic policies, limiting the scope of justice for its citizens. For example, the refusal to view healthcare as a human right, unlike in many other developed countries, illustrates the gap between America's civil rights protections and broader human rights standards.

Why the Distinction Matters

While civil rights are essential for ensuring legal equality within a specific nation, they do not always encompass the full range of human rights necessary for an individual's dignity, safety, and well-being. The fight for civil rights in America, particularly for Black Americans, has achieved significant victories, but it has often been limited to securing equality within an existing system that still perpetuates economic and social inequalities.

To achieve true justice and equality, the U.S. must expand its focus from merely securing civil rights to recognizing and enforcing universal human rights. This would require addressing systemic issues like poverty, healthcare access, mass incarceration, and education inequality, not just through legal reforms but through a comprehensive understanding that every individual is entitled to these basic human needs, irrespective of national policies.

Civil Rights and Assassinations:

The Civil Rights movement in America was a pivotal moment in the fight for equality and justice for Black Americans. However, this movement was met with violent resistance and dehumanizing treatment from those who opposed it.

Fred Hampton

One of the most notable incidents during this time was the murder of Fred Hampton. Fred Hampton was a prominent leader of the Black Panther Party in the late 1960s. He was known for his exceptional leadership skills and his efforts to create unity among different racial groups.

One of Hampton's most extraordinary achievements was the creation of the Rainbow Coalition, which was a coalition of various groups including Black Panthers, Puerto Rican Young Lords, and Southern White Young Patriots. The coalition worked to address issues of poverty, police brutality, and discrimination in Chicago. This coalition was a revolutionary step towards uniting people of different races and ethnicities towards a common goal of social justice.

Hampton's activism and leadership abilities were seen as a threat by the government, especially the FBI, who saw the Black Panther Party as a radical and dangerous organization. They saw Hampton's efforts to unite different groups as a threat to their power and sought to disrupt his activities. In fact, the FBI had been monitoring Hampton and the Black Panthers for a while, and they even had an informant within the party who provided them with information about Hampton's activities.

On December 4, 1969, Hampton was murdered in his sleep by police officers in a raid orchestrated by the FBI. This act of violence was an attempt to silence Hampton and the Black Panther Party's message of social justice and unity. This dehumanizing act not only took the life of a young leader but also sent a message that the government was willing to use violence to suppress any movement that challenged the status quo.

Despite his untimely death, Hampton's legacy and accomplishments continue to inspire activists to this day.

Dr. Martin Luther King Jr.

The murder of Dr. Martin Luther King Jr. is another tragic example of the dehumanizing treatment of Black Americans during the Civil Rights movement. King was a leading figure in the fight for civil rights, advocating for nonviolent resistance and racial equality. Dr. Martin Luther King Jr. was not only an advocate for civil rights but also for economic equality. He believed that racial discrimination was intertwined with economic inequality, and that both issues needed to be addressed together in order to achieve true justice.

One of King's most famous campaigns for economic justice was the Poor People's Campaign, which he launched in 1968 shortly before his assassination. The campaign was aimed at ending poverty among all Americans, regardless of race, and called for a guaranteed annual income, full employment, and affordable housing.

King also recognized the role of corporations in perpetuating discrimination and economic inequality. He called out major corporations such as Coca-Cola, Sears, and Woolworths for their discriminatory hiring practices and urged people to boycott these companies until they changed their policies.

King's activism in the area of economic justice threatened the government because it challenged the status quo and the interests of powerful corporations. It also brought together people of different races and backgrounds to demand economic equality, which could have led to a larger movement for systemic change.

King's assassination in 1968 cut short his campaign for economic justice, but his message continued to inspire people to fight for economic equality in the decades that followed. He was assassinated in 1968 in Memphis, Tennessee, by James Earl Ray, a white supremacist who opposed King's efforts to end segregation and discrimination. This act not only robbed the world of a great leader but also highlighted the dangers and risks of fighting for equality in a system that was resistant to change.

Malcolm X

Born Malcolm Little, another influential figure in the Civil Rights movement, was also a victim of dehumanizing violence. He fought tirelessly for the rights of Black Americans. He was a proponent of black nationalism and believed in the importance of self-defense, self-determination, and self-respect for Black Americans. Malcolm X's accomplishments include his work as a key figure in the Nation of Islam, where he helped to spread the teachings of the organization and promote Black pride.

Malcolm X's opposition to systemic oppression, his call for Black Americans to demand their rights and his criticism of the government and white supremacy made him a target of the FBI and other government agencies. His speeches, which were often critical of the United States government and its policies, made him a threat to those in power. The government saw him as a threat to their authority, and they were determined to stop him by any means necessary.

Despite facing constant harassment, surveillance, and even imprisonment, Malcolm X continued to fight for the rights of Black Americans. In 1965, he was assassinated while giving a speech in New York

City by members of the Nation of Islam, a group that he had previously been associated with. His death was a blow to the Black community and highlighted the dangers of speaking out against systemic oppression. He sought to unite people of all races against the forces of oppression and to create a better future for all people. Malcolm X's legacy continues to inspire those fighting for justice today.

These incidents were not isolated events, but rather part of a larger pattern of dehumanizing treatment towards Black Americans during the Civil Rights movement. Peaceful protesters were met with violence and brutality from law enforcement and white supremacists, and many were jailed, beaten, or killed for their efforts to fight for equality and justice.

The murders of Hampton, King, and Malcolm X were not just attacks on individuals, but also on the larger movement for Black liberation and economic equality. Their deaths serve as a reminder of the systemic violence and dehumanization that Black Americans have faced throughout American history and continue to face today. However, their legacies live on, inspiring new generations of activists and reminding us of the ongoing struggle for true equality and justice. Their lasting impact and example urge us as American people to progress toward Human Rights for all to restore humanity.

CHAPTER 5
A Legacy of Trauma

The legacy of slavery, systemic oppression, and dehumanizing treatment of Black Americans has had a weighty impact on their mental and emotional health. Many Black Americans today suffer from what is known as Post Traumatic Slave Syndrome, a term coined by Dr. Joy DeGruy. This syndrome is characterized by a range of symptoms including depression, anxiety, anger, and low self-esteem, among others.

Dr. Joy DeGruy's Post Traumatic Slave Syndrome (PTSS) is a theoretical framework that explores the long-lasting effects of slavery on African Americans and their descendants. PTSS suggests that the trauma of slavery, coupled with centuries of systemic racism and oppression, has been passed down through generations, manifesting in behaviors, attitudes, and psychological patterns that continue to affect Black communities today. It emphasizes that the emotional, mental, and social scars of slavery did not end with emancipation but have instead persisted, evolving into new forms of trauma.

Key Elements of PTSS

1. **Multigenerational Trauma:** PTSS is rooted in the idea that the trauma experienced by enslaved Africans in America was never fully ad-

dressed, healed, or resolved. The violent dehumanization, exploitation, and brutality inflicted on Black people during slavery created deep psychological wounds. These traumas were passed down through generations, affecting not only those who were directly enslaved but also their descendants.

2. **Adaptations to Oppression:** Dr. DeGruy explains that many behaviors seen within Black communities today can be understood as adaptations to an oppressive environment. During slavery, Black people developed coping mechanisms to survive the constant threats of violence, control, and dehumanization. These survival strategies, such as hypervigilance or internalized self-hate, persisted even after slavery ended, as systemic racism and discriminatory practices continued to oppress African Americans through mechanisms like Jim Crow laws, segregation, and mass incarceration.

3. **Cognitive Dissonance and Historical Denial:** DeGruy also addresses the cognitive dissonance experienced by White Americans in justifying slavery and its aftermath. This denial of responsibility, coupled with the glorification of the past, continues to prevent honest discussions about the legacy of slavery, leaving its effects unresolved. As a result, both Black and White Americans suffer from the consequences of a society that refuses to reckon fully with its history.

4. **Internalized Racism and Low Self-Esteem:** PTSS examines how systemic racism has led to internalized racism among Black people. Dr. DeGruy argues that centuries of being told that Black lives are worth less have resulted in feelings of inferiority, low self-esteem, and distrust within Black communities. These psychological impacts are seen in issues such as colorism, where lighter skin is often valued over darker skin due to internalized racial hierarchies.

5. **Intergenerational Transmission of Trauma:** Through behaviors, language, and cultural expressions, trauma from slavery and subsequent oppression is passed from one generation to the next. Families and communities may unconsciously perpetuate trauma through child-rearing

practices, communication styles, and survival instincts, all of which are rooted in the historical trauma of slavery.

Dr. Joy DeGruy's Post Traumatic Slave Syndrome offers a powerful framework for understanding the enduring legacy of slavery in the lives of African Americans today. It highlights the need for societal healing through education, acknowledgment of historical trauma, and efforts to address systemic racism. We will highlight her Pathways to Healing when we discuss healing and reconciliation later in this book. By understanding PTSS, individuals and communities can begin to break the cycle of trauma and move towards greater well-being and empowerment.

The trauma of slavery and its legacy has been passed down through generations, manifesting in various forms of physical and psychological distress. The trauma has been compounded by ongoing systemic oppression and discrimination, which has limited opportunities for Black Americans to thrive and succeed. The dehumanizing treatment of Black Americans has created a sense of learned helplessness and hopelessness, leading to a feeling of powerlessness and despair.

These issues have been further exacerbated by a lack of access to mental health resources and support. Many Black Americans face significant barriers in accessing quality healthcare, including mental health services, due to systemic racism and discrimination within the healthcare system.

Overall, the trauma and dehumanization experienced by Black Americans over centuries have had a lasting impact on their mental and emotional health. It is crucial that steps are taken to address the systemic issues at the root of this trauma, and to provide necessary resources and support to help individuals heal and overcome these challenges.

Dehumanized Mindset of White American Slave Owners and its Ongoing Legacy

The mindset of the White American slave owner was deeply influenced by the economic system of slavery, which required them to view enslaved people as property rather than as human beings. This dehumanization of enslaved people allowed slave owners to rationalize the brutal treatment and exploitation of the people they enslaved. This was further cemented as this mindset was passed on to their children to perpetuate their status and keep the family business going.

One way in which slave owners dehumanized enslaved people was by denying their basic humanity. Enslaved people were often referred to as "property" or "chattel," reducing them to the status of a commodity rather than a person. This allowed slave owners to justify the inhumane treatment of enslaved people, including physical abuse, forced labor, and the separation of families.

Another way in which slave owners dehumanized enslaved people was by promoting racial stereotypes and myths. Enslaved people were often portrayed as lazy, unintelligent, and lacking in moral character, which further reinforced the idea that they were not fully human. These stereotypes also served to justify the continued subjugation of enslaved people and to reinforce the superiority of white people.

The mindset of the American slave owner had a lasting impact on American society, including the continued dehumanization of Black people even after slavery was abolished. The legacy of this mindset can be seen in the ongoing racial inequality and systemic racism that persists in America today. It is important to recognize and confront the dehumanizing beliefs and attitudes that underlie these injustices in order to create a more just and equitable society for all.

The dehumanizing mindset of the American slave owner not only led to the dehumanization of enslaved people, but it also had a profound effect on the slave owners themselves. In order to view enslaved people as property, slave owners had to convince themselves that their human rights and dignity did not matter. That they, the enslaved people, were not human at all.

This type of thinking created a moral and psychological disconnect between the slave owner and their own humanity. It allowed them to engage in inhumane practices and treat people as property, without feeling a sense of guilt nor remorse. This detachment from humanity created a cycle of dehumanization that affected both enslaved people and slave owners alike.

Furthermore, the economic reliance on slavery as a profitable industry further fueled this dehumanization. Slave owners viewed enslaved people as nothing more than property to be bought and sold for profit. This commodification of human beings further reinforced the idea that enslaved people were not fully human and did not deserve the same rights and privileges as White people. Therefore, to ensure the continuance of their generational business model and wealth, slave owners had to teach this mindset to their children. This was necessary to preserve their economic and social way of life.

The dehumanizing mindset of the White American slave owner had long-lasting effects on their own psychological well-being and morality as well as their families. It contributed to a culture of violence and oppression that continues to affect American society today. It is important to acknowledge this history and work towards healing and reconciliation in order to move towards a more just and equitable society.

Slave Insurance

Slave insurance was a type of policy that was purchased by slave owners in America to protect their financial investment in enslaved people. It was first introduced in the late 18th century and became more popular as the number of enslaved people increased in the United States.

Slave insurance policies were designed to protect the slave owner's investment in case the enslaved person became sick, injured, or died. These policies provided coverage for various scenarios, including death from natural causes, accidents, or even injuries inflicted by other enslaved people. The policies also covered the loss of income that would result from the slave's inability to work due to illness or injury.

One of the key aspects of slave insurance was the valuation of the enslaved person. To purchase an insurance policy, slave owners had to provide detailed information about the enslaved person, including their age, sex, occupation, and health status. This information was used to determine the value of the enslaved person, which was the basis for the insurance coverage.

Slave insurance policies were sold by various companies, including the New York Life Insurance Company, Aetna Insurance Company, and others. Some of these companies continued to sell slave insurance policies even after the abolition of slavery, as the policies were still needed to protect the financial investment of those who had purchased enslaved people before abolition.

The use of slave insurance highlights the ways in which enslaved people were viewed as property and treated as commodities to be bought and sold for profit. The dehumanization of enslaved people was not only evident in the brutal treatment they endured, but also in the ways in which they were treated as mere financial assets.

Passing on the mindset

The mindset that slave owners had to teach their children was one of superiority and entitlement. They were taught that they were inherently better than Black people and that it was their God-given right to own them. This mentality was deeply ingrained in the culture and passed down from generation to generation.

The effects of this dehumanizing mindset on White Americans today are complex and far-reaching. On one hand, many White Americans have been taught to view themselves as superior to Black people, leading to systemic racism and discrimination in many areas of life. This can manifest in everything from hiring practices to housing discrimination to the criminal justice system and even the American legislative system.

On the other hand, many White Americans today are also struggling with the guilt and shame of their ancestors' actions. They may feel personally responsible for the injustices that were inflicted on Black people and feel a sense of obligation to make amends. This can lead to feelings of helplessness and hopelessness, as they grapple with the enormity of the problem and the difficulty of finding meaningful solutions.

Moreover, the legacy of slavery and systemic oppression has left deep scars on both Black and White Americans, and healing will require a concerted effort from all members of society to acknowledge and address the trauma that has been inflicted.

Eugenics

Eugenics is a concept that refers to the practice of selectively breeding individuals to improve the overall genetic makeup of a population. In the late 19th and early 20th centuries, eugenics gained popularity among some White Americans as a means of promoting the supposed superiority of the White race over other races, particularly Black Americans.

Eugenicists believed that certain traits, such as intelligence, beauty, and physical strength, were hereditary and that by selectively breeding individuals with these traits, the overall genetic quality of the population could be improved. However, this led to the belief that certain individuals, particularly those who were considered "feeble-minded" or "mentally deficient," should be prevented from reproducing to prevent their supposed "inferior" genes from being passed on to future generations.

In practice, this led to the forced sterilization of many Black Americans and other minority groups, particularly those who were living in poverty or who were considered to be "unfit" by eugenicists. These forced sterilizations, which continued into the mid-20th century, were carried out under the guise of improving the genetic quality of the American population, but in reality, they were a means of further dehumanizing and controlling Black Americans.

The impact of eugenics on American society today is significant. The legacy of eugenics has perpetuated a belief in the supposed superiority of the White race over other races and has contributed to ongoing racial disparities in areas such as healthcare, education, and criminal justice. Furthermore, the forced sterilization of Black Americans and other minority groups is a clear violation of their human rights and has left a lasting trauma on the affected individuals and their families.

It is important to acknowledge and address the harmful legacy of eugenics in American history, and to work towards creating a more just and equitable society for all individuals, regardless of race or background. This requires ongoing education and awareness about the harmful effects of eugenics, and a commitment to dismantling the systemic structures of oppression that continue to impact Black Americans and other minority groups today.

Origins of Policing in America

The origins of policing in America can be traced back to the slave patrols of the 1700s. These patrols were made up of white men who were tasked with maintaining control over the enslaved population, preventing slave rebellions, and enforcing the laws that governed slavery.

The dehumanizing effects of these patrols were many. Enslaved people were treated as property rather than human beings and were subject to brutal punishments for even minor infractions. The patrols also had the power to arrest and detain any Black person they deemed suspicious, which often resulted in innocent people being kidnapped and sold into slavery.

After the abolition of slavery, the same principles of control and domination were used against newly freed Black people. The Black Codes, which were a series of laws enacted by Southern states after the Civil War, restricted the movement and employment opportunities of Black people and gave law enforcement even more power to arrest and detain them.

Throughout the 20th century, police brutality and racial profiling continued to be major issues for Black and brown people in America. From the Civil Rights movement to the present day, the disproportionate use of force against these communities has led to countless deaths and traumatic experiences.

Today, the impact of policing on Black and brown communities is still being felt. Many people of color do not feel safe in the presence of police officers, and incidents of police violence and discrimination continue to make headlines. The dehumanizing effects of policing in America are an ongoing issue that must be addressed and dismantled in order to create a more just and equitable society. However, this problem will be a very challenging endeavor due to the fact that policing and convict leasing have become a very profitable system in America.

Convict Leasing and the American Criminals Justice System

Convict leasing was a practice that began in the late 19th century after the abolition of slavery in the United States. It involved the leasing of prisoners, most of whom were Black or Brown, to plantation owners and corporations for labor. This practice was another form of dehumanization and exploitation of Black and Brown people.

After the Civil War, many Southern states implemented a range of measures to criminalize Black people and maintain white supremacy. These measures included "Black Codes," which criminalized a range of activities such as unemployment, vagrancy, and loitering. The penalties for violating these laws were harsh, and the state often used these laws to imprison Black people and lease them out to plantation owners and corporations. This was and is completely legal due to the afore mentioned loophole in the 13th Amendment which reads, "except as a punishment for crime."

Convict leasing was a profitable business for Southern states and plantation owners. It allowed them to continue to exploit Black people for their labor without having to pay them. The prisoners were often subject to inhumane working conditions, long hours, and physical abuse. They were also denied basic human rights such as medical care, decent food, and proper clothing. This practice still continues today.

The impact of convict leasing and the criminal justice system on Black and Brown people is still felt today. The system is disproportionately harsh on people of color, with Black people being more likely to be stopped, searched, arrested, and sentenced to longer terms than White people. The system also perpetuates a cycle of poverty and marginalization, with people of color being more likely to be unemployed, underemployed, and living in poverty.

In recent years, there have been efforts to reform the criminal justice system and address the impact of convict leasing on Black and Brown communities. However, the legacy of this system continues to be felt, and it will take significant work to dismantle the structural racism that underpins it.

White Rage

The term "White Rage" was first coined by Carol Anderson, a professor of African American Studies at Emory University, in her book of the same name. It refers to the systemic and historical pattern of white backlash against progress made by Black people in America, particularly in response to advancements towards racial equality.

Throughout history, whenever black people have made significant strides towards achieving political, social, and economic equality, there has been a pattern of white resistance in the form of violence, policy changes, and legal battles. For example, during the Reconstruction era after the Civil War, when black people were granted the right to vote and hold political office, there was a surge of violence by white supremacist groups like the Ku Klux Klan, who sought to intimidate and suppress black voters.

Similarly, during the Civil Rights Movement of the 1950s and 60s, there was a violent response from White supremacists to peaceful protests and demonstrations. This included the bombings of Black churches and homes, the murder of civil rights activists like Medgar Evers and Emmett Till, and the violent suppression of peaceful protests like Bloody Sunday in Selma, Alabama.

In more recent times, we can see White Rage manifested in the backlash against the election of the first Black President, Barack Obama. This was seen in the rise of the Tea Party movement, which sought to undermine President Obama's agenda and perpetuated racist stereotypes about him and his family. We can also see another example of White Rage in the resurgence of White nationalist groups and the increase in hate crimes against marginalized communities.

The dehumanizing effects of White Rage are pervasive and can be seen in the continued systemic oppression of Black and brown people in America. It reinforces the idea that Black people are not deserving of the same rights and opportunities as White people, and that any progress made towards equality is a threat to White power and privilege.

Ultimately, the concept of White Rage highlights the need for continued efforts towards racial justice and equality in America. It is important to recognize the patterns of historical and systemic oppression that have led us to where we are today, and to actively work towards rebuilding those systems and creating a more just and equitable society for all. If these patterns are not acknowledged, addressed, and changed, we could be doomed to the unfortunate result of increased rage ultimately coming to a violent end.

CHAPTER 6

Media, Representation, and Education

Media Portrayal of White and Black Americans:

Throughout American history, the media has played a significant role in shaping public opinion and perpetuating harmful stereotypes about both White and Black people. From the minstrel shows of the 19th century to the portrayal of Black individuals as criminals and gangsters in modern media, these stereotypes have contributed to the dehumanization and mistreatment of Black Americans.

One of the most significant examples of harmful media portrayals is the use of blackface in minstrel shows in the 19th century. White performers would use makeup to darken their skin and exaggerate their features to portray Black people as lazy, ignorant, inferior, and as savages who were and ever-present danger to White people. These performances reinforced the idea that Black people were subhuman and contributed to the normalization of racism.

In the 20th century, media portrayals of Black people continued to be negative and often reinforced stereotypes. Black individuals were often portrayed as criminals, drug addicts, or gang members, perpetuating the idea that they were inherently violent and dangerous. This contributed to the acceptance of over-policing and mistreatment of Black people by law enforcement and the criminal justice system.

On the other hand, media portrayals of White people often focused on their intelligence, morality, civility, and superiority. This reinforced the idea that White people were the norm and superior to other races, including Black people.

These harmful media portrayals have had a lasting impact on American society, contributing to the dehumanization and mistreatment of Black Americans. They have also contributed to the development of implicit biases and racial stereotypes that continue to influence how Black people are perceived and treated today.

It is essential to recognize the harmful impact of media portrayals and work to create more accurate and positive representations of all races and ethnicities. This includes hiring more diverse writers, directors, and producers to ensure that a wider range of perspectives is represented in media. It also involves holding media companies accountable for perpetuating harmful stereotypes and encouraging them to make more responsible choices in their content.

Diction matters

Another way the media has contributed to the dehumanization of Black Americans is through its use of specific diction and language to portray White people more positively and Black people more negatively.

One example of this is the use of the word "thug" to describe Black people who engage in criminal behavior. The term is often used to justify violence against Black people and to criminalize their behavior, even when it is non-violent. In contrast, White people who engage in similar behavior are often described using less negative language, such as "troubled" or "misunderstood." After the January 6th insurrection, many media outlets and politicians called the insurrectionists "patriots."

Another example is the use of the word "riot" to describe Black people protesting against systemic racism and police brutality. The term is often used to suggest that Black people are inherently violent and that their protests are a threat to public safety. In contrast, White people who protest against issues such as COVID-19 restrictions or the deadly Unite the Right Rally are often described as exercising their rights to free speech and peaceful assembly.

The media has also used specific diction to reinforce harmful stereotypes about Black people, such as describing them as "lazy," "criminal," or "violent." In contrast, White people are often described using more positive language, such as "hardworking," "innocent," or "heroic."

Specific Media Cases

The contrast in diction used by media outlets when discussing high-profile cases involving people like George Floyd, Philando Castile, George Zimmerman, and Kyle Rittenhouse highlights a deeper pattern of racial bias and differential treatment in media narratives. This language disparity often perpetuates stereotypes and reinforces societal attitudes that dehumanize Black individuals while portraying White individuals more sympathetically. Below is a breakdown of some of the common contrasts in media diction used when covering these cases:

1. Victim vs. Suspect Language

- **George Floyd** *(Black victim of police violence)*:
  - Diction: Often referred to as a "suspect" or his past legal issues were highlighted.
  - Examples: "George Floyd had a criminal record," "Floyd was suspected of using counterfeit money."
  - Effect: This type of language dehumanizes the victim, implying that his death was, in some way, justified or deserved based on his past actions or alleged crime, despite the fact that this should not have led to his murder.
- **Kyle Rittenhouse** *(White shooter who killed two men at a protest)*:
  - Diction: Described as a "teenager" or "young man" who was "protecting property" or "acting in self-defense."
  - Examples: "Rittenhouse, a teen with aspirations of being a police officer," "A patriot protecting businesses."
  - Effect: This diction evokes sympathy and casts Rittenhouse in a positive light, positioning him as someone who made a mistake or acted in good faith rather than as a criminal.

2. Criminalization vs. Humanization

- **Philando Castile** *(Black victim of police violence)*:
  - Diction: The media sometimes referred to his legal possession of a firearm as suspicious, emphasizing his "car smelled of marijuana" or how he was "a suspect in previous police reports."

- Examples: "Castile had been stopped multiple times before" or "He appeared nervous when reaching for his wallet."
- Effect: This diction criminalizes the victim even when they were compliant or did not pose a real threat. It emphasizes guilt or suspicion.

- **George Zimmerman** *(White-Hispanic shooter of Trayvon Martin)*:
  - Diction: Zimmerman was portrayed as a neighborhood watch volunteer who "feared for his life" when he shot Trayvon Martin.
  - Examples: "Zimmerman was protecting the neighborhood from break-ins" or "He acted in self-defense after being attacked."
  - Effect: This humanizes Zimmerman by framing him as a protector who acted out of necessity. The emphasis is placed on his perception of danger rather than his role in escalating the confrontation.

3. Passive Voice vs. Active Voice

- **George Floyd:**
  - Diction: Passive voice often used when describing his death.
  - Examples: "Floyd died after being restrained by police," "Floyd's death occurred during an arrest."
  - Effect: The use of passive language diminishes the agency of the police officers involved and obscures accountability for the action. The focus is shifted away from the active killing to the circumstances of the arrest.

- **Kyle Rittenhouse:**
  - Diction: Active voice used to describe his actions in more neutral or positive terms.
  - Examples: "Rittenhouse shot and killed two men during a protest," "He acted to protect himself."
  - Effect: The active voice emphasizes that Rittenhouse's actions were deliberate and often frames them as justifiable in self-defense, giving him more agency and control over the narrative.

4. Racialized Adjectives and Implicit Bias

- **Black Victims** *(e.g., Floyd, Castile, Martin)*:
  - Diction: Words like "agitated," "combative," "threatening," or even physical descriptors like "large," "muscular" were used.
  - Examples: "Floyd appeared agitated during the arrest," "Martin, wearing a hoodie, appeared suspicious in the neighborhood."
  - Effect: These adjectives emphasize perceived aggression or danger, reinforcing stereotypes of Black men as violent, aggressive, or inherently dangerous, regardless of their actual behavior.

- **White Suspects** *(e.g., Zimmerman, Rittenhouse)*:
  - o Diction: Words like "confused," "frightened," "young," or "inexperienced" were used.
  - o Examples: "Rittenhouse, a confused teenager, was caught in the chaos of protests," "Zimmerman was simply following his duties as a neighborhood watchman."
  - o Effect: These adjectives frame the White suspects as innocent, naive, or overwhelmed by circumstances, invoking sympathy and justifying their actions.

5. Focus on Individual Accountability vs. Systemic Issues

- **George Floyd:**
  - o Diction: Media narratives often focus on Floyd's individual actions or circumstances, such as drug use or previous encounters with the law.
  - o Examples: "Floyd was high on fentanyl at the time of his arrest," "Floyd's criminal past came to light."
  - o Effect: This individualizes the issue, suggesting that Floyd's actions were largely responsible for his own death, rather than acknowledging the broader issue of systemic racism in policing.
- **Kyle Rittenhouse:**
  - o Diction: Media frequently framed Rittenhouse as a product of his environment, highlighting external factors such as "violent protests" or "chaos."
  - o Examples: "Rittenhouse was swept up in the violence of the protests," "He traveled to Kenosha to defend businesses."
  - o Effect: This shifts blame away from the individual and onto the broader social unrest, portraying Rittenhouse as a victim of circumstances rather than a perpetrator.

6. Descriptive Imagery: Hero vs. Victim

- **Kyle Rittenhouse:**
  - o Imagery: Often depicted with a sense of duty, sometimes with patriotic undertones.
  - o Examples: Images of him cleaning graffiti, attending court clean-shaven, and discussions about his aspirations to be a police officer.
  - o Effect: This imagery serves to portray Rittenhouse as someone with good intentions, fostering a positive public perception.
- **George Floyd:**
  - o Imagery: Early images of Floyd were often from his arrest or moments of distress.

- Examples: Images of Floyd pinned under the officer's knee, or mug-shots from previous arrests.
- Effect: These images dehumanize Floyd by associating him with criminality or weakness, reinforcing the narrative of him being a suspect rather than a victim.

The impact of this biased language is significant. It reinforces negative stereotypes about Black people, perpetuates systemic racism, and contributes to the dehumanization of Black people in American society. It can also lead to the justification of discriminatory policies and practices, such as racial profiling and unequal treatment under the law.

The diction and imagery used by the media when reporting on cases involving Black and White individuals are not just reflections of racial biases—they actively shape public perception. The use of sympathetic language for White suspects like Kyle Rittenhouse and criminalizing language for Black victims like George Floyd or Philando Castile reflects a long-standing societal tendency to dehumanize Black individuals while casting White individuals in a more favorable light. This disparity not only perpetuates stereotypes but also reinforces systemic inequalities, which continue to influence how justice is administered in the United States.

Overall, it is crucial to be aware of the language used in the media and to challenge harmful stereotypes and biases whenever possible. By doing so, we can work towards a more just and equitable society for all.

Discriminatory Educational Practices:

The American government did not explicitly make it illegal for enslaved people to read, but many slave states did pass laws prohibiting enslaved individuals from learning to read and write. The rationale behind these laws was rooted in the fear that an educated enslaved population would be more likely to rebel and resist their oppression. Slave owners recognized the power that knowledge could provide to their enslaved individuals, and they sought to deny them that power in order to maintain control over them.

One example of such a law was the North Carolina Slave Code of 1831, which made it illegal to teach enslaved individuals to read and write, punishable by a fine or imprisonment. The code justified this restriction on the grounds that it was necessary to prevent "the evils arising from an unrestricted intercourse between the two races." Similar laws were passed in other states such as Georgia and Virginia.

The prohibition of education for enslaved people was a dehumanizing measure that denied them the basic human right of access to knowledge and perpetuated their subjugation. The legacy of this systemic oppression can still be seen in the persistent educational achievement gap that exists today between Black and White Americans.

Dehumanization in the American Education System

Dehumanization, the process of stripping individuals or groups of their humanity, has been deeply embedded in various facets of American society, and its legacy within the education system is particularly profound. The American education system, since its inception, has often mirrored the racial, social, and economic inequalities present in the broader society. For generations, it has been a key arena where dehumanizing policies and practices have been institutionalized, especially concerning Black, Indigenous, and other marginalized communities. From segregation and discriminatory curriculum to standardized testing and funding inequities, dehumanization in education has contributed to a cycle of disenfranchisement that continues to affect students today.

1. Segregation and Unequal Access to Education

One of the most explicit examples of dehumanization in the American education system was the segregation of schools. Under the doctrine of "separate but equal," upheld by the 1896 Plessy v. Ferguson decision, Black and White students were kept in separate schools, but the resources, facilities, and educational quality afforded to Black students were far from equal. This segregation, particularly in the Jim Crow South, created a system where Black children were taught in dilapidated buildings with limited materials, underpaid teachers, and inadequate access to basic resources like textbooks, laboratories, or libraries.

- Dehumanizing Impact: Segregation reinforced the idea that Black students were inherently inferior and unworthy of the same opportunities as their White peers. This institutionalized inequality sent the message that Black children did not deserve or were not capable of the same quality of education, thereby stunting their intellectual and social development.

Even after the landmark Brown v. Board of Education ruling in 1954, which declared segregation unconstitutional, resistance to desegregation was fierce. White communities often responded with hostility, and in many cases, schools were slow to integrate, leading to continued disparities in educational opportunities. Additionally, the creation of White private academies and the redrawing of school district lines to maintain predominantly White schools furthered the dehumanization of Black students.

2. The Hidden Curriculum and Whitewashing of History

The content of what is taught in schools has also played a significant role in dehumanizing marginalized communities. The "hidden curriculum" in many American schools has perpetuated a narrative that centers White achievement, glosses over or omits the contributions of Black, Indigenous, and other minority groups, and portrays these communities in a negative or inferior light.

- For example, textbooks have long framed Christopher Columbus as a heroic explorer, downplaying or ignoring his role in the enslavement and decimation of Native American populations. Similarly, the horrors of slavery have been minimized, sometimes framed as a "necessary evil" or as an institution that was less brutal than it actually was. This distorted narrative teaches students of color, particularly Black and Indigenous students, that their history and culture are of lesser value, which in turn can affect their self-esteem, sense of belonging, and academic achievement.

- Dehumanizing Impact: The erasure or misrepresentation of non-White histories reinforces the notion that only White experiences, achievements, and perspectives are central to American identity. This narrative not only alienates students of color but also prevents White students from understanding the full, nuanced history of the country, which continues to perpetuate racial biases and divisions.

The work of groups like the Daughters of the Confederacy has contributed to this whitewashing of history. For decades, they were instrumental in shaping the way the Civil War, slavery, and Reconstruction were taught in Southern schools, emphasizing the "Lost Cause" myth, which glorified the Confederacy and minimized the role of slavery as the cause of the war. This curriculum instilled a distorted sense of history in generations of students and further dehumanized Black Americans by downplaying their suffering and contributions to the nation.

The United Daughters of the Confederacy (UDC) and Moms for Liberty are two organizations that have played influential roles in shaping American education, particularly in relation to the teaching of history. Though separated by over a century, these organizations share similar goals in controlling narratives around American history and reinforcing ideologies that obscure or diminish the reality of racial oppression, particularly slavery, the Civil War, and the Civil Rights Movement. Both groups have had significant impacts on how history is taught in schools, which continues to influence the collective understanding of America's past.

The United Daughters of the Confederacy: Rewriting History

Founded in 1894, the United Daughters of the Confederacy (UDC) was initially formed as a Southern women's organization dedicated to preserving the memory of Confederate soldiers and their "lost cause." However, the UDC went beyond memorialization and became heavily involved in shaping the way the Civil War, slavery, and the Confederacy were remembered and taught. One of the UDC's most significant accomplishments was its influence over educational content in the early 20th century.

Influence on Education

The UDC's work was pivotal in promoting what became known as the "Lost Cause" myth—the idea that the Civil War was fought over states' rights rather than slavery, and that the Confederacy was a noble but doomed cause. Their impact on education included:

A. **Textbook Control:** The UDC influenced the content of textbooks, especially in Southern states. Through pressure on state education boards, they ensured that textbooks downplayed the brutality of slavery, portrayed enslaved people as content, and minimized the role of slavery as a cause of the Civil War. Instead, the UDC promoted a narrative of the Confederacy as a heroic defense of Southern culture.

B. **Erecting Monuments and Memorials:** The UDC erected hundreds of Confederate monuments across the South, many of which were placed in front of schools and government buildings. These monuments were not just memorials to the dead, but powerful symbols that reinforced the idea of White supremacy and the righteousness of the Confederate cause. These symbols helped shape the cultural and educational environment in which Southern children learned about the past.

C. **"Southern Values" Curriculum:** Through local school boards, the UDC helped to establish a curriculum that focused on teaching Southern values, which often included a sanitized version of slavery and Reconstruction. By controlling what students learned in school, the UDC aimed to foster a sense of pride in Confederate heritage while also promoting a version of history that excluded the voices and experiences of enslaved Black Americans.

Dehumanizing Impact on Black Americans

The UDC's efforts to rewrite history through textbooks and monuments dehumanized Black Americans by portraying them as passive figures in their own history. By promoting the idea that slavery was benign, and that enslaved people were loyal to their enslavers, the UDC perpetuated harmful stereotypes that still linger today. Their version of history erased the brutality and violence of slavery and marginalized the contributions of Black Americans to the nation's development. Moreover, by glorifying the Confederacy, the UDC promoted a narrative that implicitly (and sometimes explicitly) suggested that White supremacy was a natural and justified social order.

Moms for Liberty: A Modern Movement of Dehumanization

Moms for Liberty, founded in 2021, is a right-wing group that focuses on parental rights, particularly in relation to public education. They have become known for challenging what they consider to be "woke" or progressive educational agendas, including teachings about race, gender, and American history. Like the UDC, Moms for Liberty advocates for controlling how certain topics are presented in schools, particularly those related to the history of slavery, the Civil Rights Movement, and systemic racism.

Similar Tactics in Controlling Educational Narratives

Moms for Liberty uses many of the same tactics as the UDC to shape public education:

A. **Book Bans and Curriculum Challenges:** Moms for Liberty has been at the forefront of efforts to ban books that deal with race, gender, sexuality, and systemic inequality. In their view, many of these books promote "divisive" or "anti-American" ideas. This echoes the UDC's earlier efforts to censor textbooks and control curriculum to avoid topics that highlighted the brutal realities of slavery and the Confederacy's role in upholding racial oppression.

B. **Legislative Pressure:** Moms for Liberty has successfully lobbied for the passage of laws in several states that restrict how teachers can discuss topics like racism, White privilege, and systemic inequality. These laws, often referred to as "anti-CRT" (Critical Race Theory) laws, seek to prevent students from learning about the structural and historical nature of racism in America. This mirrors the UDC's influence over state education boards and local curricula to ensure that students were not exposed to narratives that challenged the Lost Cause myth.

C. **Fostering Cultural Backlash:** Both organizations operate in times of cultural backlash. The UDC rose to prominence during the Jim Crow era, when White Southerners sought to reassert White supremacy after the end of Reconstruction. Similarly, Moms for Liberty has emerged in response to growing movements for racial justice, particularly following the protests after George Floyd's murder in 2020. Both groups present themselves as defenders of "traditional values" in the face of what they see as a radical reimagining of American history.

The Dehumanizing Impact of Both Movements

Both the UDC and Moms for Liberty have contributed to dehumanizing marginalized groups by controlling the historical narrative taught to children. In the case of the UDC, their rewriting of history erased the brutality of slavery and glorified the Confederacy, reinforcing a narrative of White supremacy. This had a profound impact on generations of students, particularly in the South, who grew up learning a distorted version of history that downplayed or ignored the suffering of Black Americans.

Moms for Liberty's efforts to limit discussions of systemic racism and discrimination in schools have a similar dehumanizing effect. By preventing students from learning about the full scope of American history, including the ways in which racism has shaped the nation's institutions, they reinforce the idea that these issues are either unimportant or nonexistent. This erasure of historical truths marginalizes the experiences of Black, Brown, and Indigenous Americans, while reinforcing the notion that the discomfort of White students or parents is more important than teaching the truth.

The Ongoing Struggle for Historical Accuracy and Equity

The efforts of the UDC and Moms for Liberty to control the narrative of American history are part of a larger struggle over how the nation understands itself and its past. Both groups seek to promote a version of history that erases or minimizes the experiences of marginalized groups, particularly Black Americans, while reinforcing a version of American exceptionalism that ignores systemic inequality. This has long-term consequences for how students—especially White students—understand their place in the world and their relationship to issues of race, privilege, and power.

Addressing the dehumanizing impacts of these groups requires a commitment to teaching accurate, inclusive history that reflects the complexity of the American experience. It means confronting the uncomfortable truths about the country's past, including its legacy of slavery, segregation, and ongoing systemic racism. Without this commitment, future generations will continue to be misinformed about the realities of race and power in America, perpetuating cycles of inequality and dehumanization.

The Legacy of Historical Erasure

The influence of the United Daughters of the Confederacy and Moms for Liberty represents a continued effort to whitewash American history and suppress the stories of marginalized communities. While the UDC sought to legitimize the Confederacy and rewrite the history of the Civil War and Reconstruction, Moms for Liberty is attempting to prevent honest discussions about race, power, and inequality in today's classrooms. Both movements reflect a broader fear of confronting our country's past and its ongoing struggles with racial injustice.

In order to build a more equitable and just future, it is essential that the American education system resists these dehumanizing forces and embraces a full, honest accounting of history—one that includes the voices, experiences, and contributions of all Americans, not just those in power.

3. Disproportionate Discipline and the School-to-Prison Pipeline

A modern manifestation of dehumanization in the American education system is the disproportionate discipline of Black and Brown students. Studies have consistently shown that students of color, particularly Black students, are far more likely to be suspended, expelled, or referred to law enforcement for the same behaviors that result in more lenient punishment for their White peers. This discriminatory practice has come to be known as the "school-to-prison pipeline."

- Dehumanizing Impact: This form of discipline frames Black and Brown children as inherently more dangerous or less capable of being reformed, reinforcing negative stereotypes about their behavior and worth. The over-policing of students of color within schools often mirrors the over-policing they experience in their communities, reinforcing the notion that they are criminal by nature. This leads to long-term detrimental effects, such as lower graduation rates, higher dropout rates, and increased likelihood of interaction with the criminal justice system.

4. Standardized Testing and Cultural Bias

Standardized testing has also played a role in dehumanizing marginalized students. These tests, which are often used to determine a student's academic ability, placement, or future success, have historically been biased in favor of White, middle-class students. The content of many standardized tests assumes a certain level of cultural knowledge or life experience that may not be shared by students from different racial, ethnic, or socioeconomic backgrounds.

Standardized testing has been used in America for decades as a means of measuring a student's knowledge and aptitude. However, it has also been used as a tool for exclusion rather than inclusion, particularly for Black and brown students.

One of the earliest examples of standardized testing being used in a dehumanizing way was during the early 20th century when the eugenics movement was gaining popularity. Eugenicists believed that certain races and ethnic groups were genetically inferior and therefore, less intelligent than White Americans. As a result, they used standardized tests to prove their point and justify policies such as segregation and forced sterilization.

During the 1920s and 1930s, intelligence testing was used to exclude Black and brown students from higher education. The SAT, which was first administered in 1926, was designed to identify the best and brightest students for admission to elite universities. However, the test was based on a White, middle-class perspective, and questions were often culturally biased, putting Black and brown students at a disadvantage. As a result, many highly qualified students were denied admission to top schools.

Standardized testing has also been used as a means of tracking students into different levels of education. In the mid-20th century, IQ tests were used to segregate Black and brown students into lower tracks, which often led to lower-quality education and limited opportunities. This system perpetuated the idea that Black and brown students were less intelligent and worthy of a lesser education.

Today, standardized testing continues to have a dehumanizing impact on Black and brown students. Studies have shown that standardized tests are often biased against students of color and those from low-income families. These biases can lead to lower test scores, which can limit opportunities for higher education and future success.

Furthermore, standardized testing often fails to account for the diverse experiences and knowledge that students bring to the classroom. Black and brown students who come from different backgrounds and have different life experiences are often at a disadvantage on standardized tests that are designed from a White, middle-class perspective.

Standardized testing has been used as a tool for exclusion rather than inclusion, perpetuating the dehumanizing treatment of Black and brown students in America. It is crucial to recognize these biases and work towards a more equitable education system that values and celebrates the diversity of all students.

- Dehumanizing Impact: The reliance on standardized testing as a measure of intelligence or potential disproportionately labels Black, Brown, and low-income students as "less intelligent" or "underperforming." This contributes to tracking systems that place these students in lower-level classes, reducing their access to advanced coursework and limiting their opportunities for academic and professional success. In essence, these tests often measure a student's familiarity with White, middle-class culture rather than their actual intellectual abilities, devaluing the experiences and knowledge of students from diverse backgrounds.

5. Funding Disparities and Resource Inequity

The funding model for public schools in America, which relies heavily on local property taxes, has created stark disparities between schools in affluent, predominantly White areas and those in low-income, predominantly Black and Brown communities. Schools in wealthier neighborhoods benefit from better facilities, more extracurricular activities, higher-paid teachers, and more comprehensive academic programs, while schools in poorer areas struggle to provide even the most basic educational resources.

- Dehumanizing Impact: This funding system perpetuates a cycle of poverty and inequality, reinforcing the notion that students in low-income, predominantly Black or Brown schools are not worthy of the same level of investment. It dehumanizes students by treating them as less deserving of quality education simply because of where they live, and it ensures that generations of students from marginalized communities are set up for failure before they even begin.

6. The Role of the "Model Minority" Myth

While dehumanization has overwhelmingly affected Black and Indigenous communities in the American education system, it has also impacted other groups, such as Asian Americans, through different mechanisms. The "model minority" myth, which stereotypes Asian Americans as inherently successful, hardworking, and high-achieving, has its own dehumanizing effects.

- Dehumanizing Impact: While on the surface this stereotype may seem positive, it dehumanizes Asian American students by reducing them to a monolithic group that is expected to perform exceptionally well, regardless of individual differences. This myth also pits Asian Americans against other communities of color, particularly Black and Latino students, reinforcing harmful racial hierarchies and undermining solidarity in the fight for educational equity.

Dehumanization and the Path Forward

Dehumanization in the American education system has taken many forms, from segregation and unequal funding to biased curricula and disproportionate discipline. These practices and policies have deeply impacted generations of marginalized students, depriving them of the opportunities and dignity that should be afforded to all children. The effects of these dehumanizing policies are still felt today in the form of persistent educational disparities, achievement gaps, and the criminalization of students of color.

Addressing this requires a fundamental rethinking of how education is structured in the United States. It involves not only desegregating schools and ensuring equitable funding but also revising curricula to reflect the true, diverse history of the nation. Moreover, it means confronting implicit biases in how students are disciplined, assessed, and treated within the classroom.

Healing the dehumanization in education means transforming the system into one that recognizes and values the humanity, culture, and potential of all students, regardless of their race, background, or socioeconomic status.

CHAPTER 7
Healing and Resolution

We have spent a lot of time on acknowledging the parts of America where dehumanization has originated, caused harm, and how it continues to negatively effect and impact America. Now let us examine the journey to healing and resolution so that we can build a stronger more positive future for America. In the remaining chapters, we will examine some healing strategies and look at some countries who have already embarked on this journey of healing. We will look at the steps they took as well as where they are today in the process. Then we will ultimately set a plan of action for America to begin our next stage of healing our humanity.

Healing the wounds of the past requires a multi-faceted approach that acknowledges the harm that has been done and works towards reconciliation, justice, and equality. Healing is often difficulty because you first must acknowledge the true history and face it head on with a plan for healing in place. Here are some possible solutions for healing the descendants of enslaved people in America:

1. **Reparations:** The United States government should provide reparations to the descendants of enslaved people. This could include monetary compensation, free education, and other resources to help address the

generational wealth gap created by slavery. Reparations are not unprecedented in the history of the United States. For example, the government provided reparations to Japanese Americans who were forcibly interned during World War II through the Civil Liberties Act of 1988, which included a formal apology and monetary compensation. Similarly, the Indian Claims Commission Act of 1946 was established to address land taken from Native American tribes, resulting in financial settlements for some tribes. Additionally, victims of the Tuskegee syphilis experiment were compensated in the 1970s after decades of medical abuse. These examples demonstrate that the U.S. has acknowledged historical wrongs and provided reparations in the past, making the case for addressing the generational harm caused by slavery both just and consistent with precedent.

2. **Education:** Schools should include accurate and comprehensive education about the history of slavery and its ongoing impacts on American society. This education should also include the contributions of enslaved people to American history and culture.

3. **Mental Health Support:** Descendants of enslaved and indigenous people may still be grappling with the intergenerational trauma of slavery and displacement. Providing mental health support services specifically targeted towards those affected by the legacy of slavery can help address this.

4. **Criminal Justice Reform:** The criminal justice system disproportionately impacts Black Americans, and this is in part due to the legacy of slavery. Reforming the criminal justice system can help address systemic inequalities and provide greater opportunities for justice and equality.

5. **Economic Opportunities:** Economic opportunities should be provided to descendants of enslaved people, such as access to affordable housing, job training, and business development resources. This can help address the wealth gap and provide greater economic stability for future generations.

6. **Political Empowerment:** Encouraging and supporting political participation and representation of descendants of enslaved people can help to ensure that their voices and needs are heard and addressed.

These solutions can help to address the ongoing impact of slavery on descendants of enslaved people in America. By acknowledging the harm that has been done and taking active steps towards reconciliation, justice, and equality, we can work towards a more just and equitable society for all. There are examples of this process that have already taken place in countries that were riddled with racism and dehumanizing practices. These countries have made significant advances to overcome their horrific histories. We should not be too proud to learn from them.

South Africa's path to healing after the apartheid:

The Truth and Reconciliation Commission (TRC) was established in South Africa in 1995 after the end of apartheid, a system of racial segregation and discrimination that had been in place for over 40 years. The TRC was tasked with investigating the human rights violations that occurred during apartheid and providing a platform for victims to share their stories and seek justice.

One of the unique aspects of the TRC was its focus on restorative justice rather than retributive justice. This meant that perpetrators of human rights violations could apply for amnesty if they fully disclosed their crimes and demonstrated that they acted with political motives.

The TRC also provided reparations to victims and their families and worked to promote national healing and reconciliation.

The TRC was not without its criticisms, as some argued that it did not go far enough in holding perpetrators accountable and that the amnesty process allowed some individuals to escape justice. However, many experts believe that the TRC played a significant role in South Africa's transition to democracy and has helped the country to move forward from its troubled past.

Today, South Africa continues to grapple with issues related to inequality, poverty, and social unrest, but the TRC's emphasis on restorative justice and national healing has had a lasting impact. The TRC helped to promote a culture of dialogue and reconciliation in South Africa, and many individuals and organizations continue to work towards these goals today. Additionally, the TRC helped to bring attention to the experiences of victims and their families, and many of the individuals who testified before the commission have since become advocates for human rights and social justice in South Africa.

There are several lessons that America can learn and apply from South Africa's Truth and Reconciliation Commission (TRC) process to begin its own healing process. Here are a few:

1. **Acknowledge the truth:** The first step towards healing is acknowledging the truth about what happened. The TRC process in South Africa allowed for victims and perpetrators to come forward and tell their stories, leading to a greater understanding of the atrocities that occurred

during apartheid. Similarly, in America, it is important to acknowledge the truth of the country's history of slavery, segregation, and discrimination against Black people, Indigenous people, and other marginalized groups.

2. **Foster a culture of empathy:** The TRC process in South Africa encouraged empathy and understanding between victims and perpetrators, as well as between different groups in society. This helped to break down barriers and create a more unified society. Similarly, in America, it is important to foster a culture of empathy and understanding between different racial and ethnic groups, and to encourage conversations and dialogue about race and racism.

3. **Provide reparations:** The TRC process in South Africa included provisions for reparations for victims of apartheid, which helped to address the economic and social disparities that had been caused by years of oppression. Similarly, in America, it is important to provide reparations for the descendants of enslaved people and to address the ongoing disparities in areas such as housing, education, and healthcare.

4. **Hold accountable those responsible for past injustices:** The TRC process in South Africa also included provisions for holding accountable those responsible for past injustices. While not everyone was prosecuted, the process helped to ensure that those who committed atrocities were held responsible for their actions. Similarly, in America, it is important to hold accountable those who have committed acts of racism and discrimination, including through the criminal justice system.

5. **Ensure meaningful participation:** Finally, the TRC process in South Africa ensured meaningful participation by victims, perpetrators, and civil society organizations, which helped to create a sense of ownership and buy-in for the process. Similarly, in America, it is important to ensure that all voices are heard and that there is meaningful participation from marginalized communities in the process of healing and reconciliation. This includes ensuring that there

are opportunities for participation from all groups, including those who may be skeptical of the process.

Lessons from Germany: Confronting Inhumane Treatment and Pursuing Healing

The history of Germany is marked by a dark chapter—the Holocaust and the systematic dehumanization and persecution of Jews during the Nazi regime. However, in the aftermath of World War II, Germany embarked on a journey of self-reflection, reconciliation, and healing. This section explores how Germany faced its inhumane treatment of Jews, the steps it took to acknowledge and atone for its past, and the ongoing progress towards healing its people.

1. **Confronting the Past:** Germany's process of healing began with a collective acknowledgment and confrontation of its dark history. The country faced the atrocities committed during the Holocaust, recognizing the dehumanization and suffering inflicted on the Jewish population. This process involved open dialogue, historical research, and memorialization efforts to ensure the truth was preserved and shared.

2. **Taking Responsibility:** Germany took collective responsibility for the actions of its past. It accepted guilt for the crimes committed, acknowledging the dehumanization of Jews as a grave violation of human rights. Political leaders, institutions, and the German people recognized the importance of taking ownership of the past and ensuring it would not be repeated.

3. **Education and Remembrance:** Germany placed great emphasis on education to ensure that future generations would understand the horrors of the Holocaust and the consequences of dehumanization. Holocaust education became a core component of the national curriculum,

teaching young Germans about the atrocities and fostering empathy, tolerance, and respect for all people.

4. **Restitution and Reparations:** Recognizing the material and psychological harm inflicted on the Jewish community, Germany committed to restitution and reparations. Compensation programs were established to provide financial support and acknowledgment to Holocaust survivors and their descendants. These efforts aimed to address the economic and emotional consequences of the dehumanization suffered.

5. **Commemoration and Memorialization:** Germany invested in commemorative initiatives to honor the victims and preserve their memory. Memorials, museums, and documentation centers were established throughout the country, serving as important spaces for remembrance, reflection, and learning. These physical reminders ensure that the dehumanization and suffering endured by Jews are never forgotten.

6. **Promoting Social Inclusion:** Germany continues to make progress in fostering social inclusion and combating discrimination. Legal protections against hate speech, antisemitism, and other forms of prejudice have been strengthened. Programs promoting intercultural dialogue, diversity, and equality are implemented to create a society that values every individual's dignity and humanity.

Germany's journey towards healing and confronting its inhumane treatment of Jews serves as an example for other nations grappling with their own histories of dehumanization. By acknowledging the past, taking responsibility, educating future generations, providing restitution, and promoting social inclusion, Germany has made significant strides in healing its people. While challenges remain, the German experience demonstrates the power of collective action, remembrance, and a commitment to preventing the repetition of dehumanizing acts.

CHAPTER 8

Pathways to Healing:

Reclaiming Humanity and Dignity for All Americans

The pathways to healing for America will definitely be a complicated path. We are made up of many people with many different life experiences, backgrounds, cultures, socio economic statuses, etc. Thus, we will examine some paths to healing facing the diverse mindsets that have been impacted by the dehumanized history of America.

Solutions for Healing the Dehumanized White American Mindset:

Healing the dehumanized mindsets of White Americans requires a multi-faceted approach that addresses the root causes of systemic oppression, racism, and prejudice. This is a massive undertaking due to the fact that not ALL White Americans share the same mindset nor the same life experiences just as ALL Black Americans have not shared the same exact life experiences. However, this speaks to the overall healing process of many mindsets in America Here are some potential solutions that could help:

1. **Education:** Education is key to understanding and dismantling systemic oppression. Schools should teach an accurate and comprehensive history that includes the perspectives and experiences of marginalized communities in all schools including majority and all White schools. This can help to address the lack of knowledge and awareness that perpetuates dehumanization and racism.

2. **Restorative justice:** Restorative justice is a model of justice that focuses on repairing harm, rather than punishment. It can provide an opportunity for White Americans to acknowledge the harm and trauma caused by their actions and behaviors, and work towards repairing the damage done.

3. **Cultural humility training:** Cultural humility training can help to build awareness and understanding of different cultures and experiences. This training can provide tools for recognizing and addressing of innate biases and promote respectful and inclusive interactions.

4. **Community-building:** Building strong communities and fostering relationships across racial and cultural lines can promote understanding and empathy. Community-based programs that facilitate communication and interaction between diverse groups can help to break down barriers and build connections. Such programs like town hall meetings held for the sole purpose of discussing topics that are polarizing and/or taboo, yet they impact everyday life and policies. These programs should follow specific civil discourse procedures and all that participate should be required to attend professional develop sessions that teach the civil discourse procedures.

5. **Personal reflection:** White Americans must also engage in personal reflection and introspection to identify and address their own biases and prejudices. This can be done through self-reflection, journaling, and seeking feedback from trusted sources.

6. **Allyship:** Allies play an important role in promoting equity and dismantling systemic oppression. White Americans can use their privilege to advocate for marginalized communities and amplify their voices.

7. **Systemic Change:** Structural changes must be made to dismantle systemic oppression and racism. This includes changes to laws and policies, as well as shifts in organizational practices and culture.

Ultimately, healing the dehumanized mindsets of White Americans requires a willingness to confront uncomfortable truths, a commitment to ongoing learning and growth, and an unwavering dedication to promoting equity and justice for all. If the willingness is there and shared amongst the entirety of America, the sky is the limit as to what we can accomplish.

Solutions for Healing the Dehumanized Capitalistic Mindset:

Corporations and businesses can take several steps to address the harm caused by their historical dehumanizing business practices in America. Here are some potential solutions:

1. **Acknowledge the harm:** The first step towards healing is acknowledging the harm that was caused. Companies can publicly acknowledge their involvement in historical injustices and commit to taking action to address the harm that was done.

2. **Provide reparations:** Companies can provide reparations to those who were harmed by their historical actions. This could include financial compensation, support for educational initiatives, or investments in community development.

3. **Invest in education:** Companies can invest in educational initiatives that help to promote greater understanding of the harm caused by their historical actions. This could include sponsoring educational programs, funding scholarships, or supporting historical research. This investment should also include the steps the companies are taking and implementing to be more inclusive and beneficial to the communities they serve.

4. **Promote diversity and inclusion:** Companies can take steps to promote greater diversity and inclusion within their organizations. This could include implementing policies to promote hiring and promotion of underrepresented groups, providing training to address bias, and fostering a culture of inclusion.

5. **Engage in advocacy:** Companies can engage in advocacy efforts to address broader societal issues related to systemic oppression and racism. This could include supporting policies that promote racial justice, speaking out against discriminatory practices, and partnering with community organizations to promote positive change.

By taking these steps, companies and businesses can begin to address the harm caused by their historical dehumanizing business practices and promote greater healing and reconciliation in society.

Solutions for Healing the Dehumanized Mindset of Black and Indigenous people:

The dehumanizing effects of centuries of systemic oppression in America have left deep psychological and cultural scars on both Black and Indigenous communities. From slavery and genocide to forced assimilation and institutionalized discrimination, generations of Black and Indigenous Americans have been subjected to relentless attacks on their identities, cultures, and humanity. The lasting impact of this history includes trauma that affects personal and collective well-being, often manifesting in a range of social and health disparities. However, healing is possible. The journey to reclaim humanity and dignity is complex, and it requires multifaceted solutions rooted in community, cultural revival, policy reform, and personal transformation. This section will explore potential pathways to healing for Black and Indigenous communities, with a focus on self-empowerment, cultural renewal, reparative justice, and trauma recovery.

1. Cultural Reclamation and Revival

One of the most powerful methods of healing for Black and Indigenous communities is reconnecting with ancestral knowledge, practices, and traditions that were deliberately suppressed. The reclamation of culture serves as an antidote to the dehumanization and erasure of history that these communities have endured. For both Black and Indigenous Americans, reclaiming cultural practices allows for a rediscovery of self-worth, identity, and resilience.

- **Revitalization of Language and Traditions:** For Indigenous communities, language holds cultural wisdom and worldview. Many Indigenous languages in the United States have faced extinction due to forced assimilation policies, such as the boarding school system. Revitalizing these languages through immersion schools, community classes, and digital resources can foster a sense of pride and continuity within Indigenous communities. For Black Americans, reconnecting with African spiritual practices, music, and storytelling traditions provides a means of reclaiming cultural identity.

- **Celebrating Historical Narratives and Heroes:** Reclaiming history by honoring the stories of resilience, resistance, and survival within Black and Indigenous communities can reshape collective identity. Teaching accurate history and celebrating heroes like Harriet Tubman, Sojourner Truth, Sitting Bull, and Wilma Mankiller empowers new generations to embrace their roots. Establishing cultural institutions, museums, and monuments dedicated to Black and Indigenous history allows communities to celebrate their legacies on their own terms.

- **Land and Food Sovereignty:** Both Black and Indigenous communities have been denied access to land, either through displacement or economic disenfranchisement. Land is deeply connected to cultural and spiritual practices, particularly for Indigenous people. Supporting land reclamation efforts, such as returning tribal lands to Indigenous control and supporting Black farming initiatives, restores agency and self-reliance. Programs that encourage food sovereignty, including community gardening and farming, can reconnect people with traditional foods and sustainable practices, offering a healing relationship with the land.

2. Community-Centered Mental Health Support

A core aspect of healing from the trauma of dehumanization is addressing the psychological toll of systemic oppression. Historical trauma—trauma passed down through generations—is real, and its effects on mental health are profound. Addressing this requires community-centered mental health approaches that recognize cultural context and historical legacies.

- **Trauma-Informed Therapy and Culturally Sensitive Counseling:** Many mental health models in the U.S. have historically failed to address the unique traumas experienced by Black and Indigenous communities. Trauma-informed therapy, particularly in the form of narrative therapy, allows individuals to process their experiences within the framework of historical trauma. For Indigenous communities, mental health programs that incorporate traditional healing practices, such as talking circles, sweat lodges, and ceremonies, can provide culturally sensitive methods for recovery. For Black Americans, therapists who are culturally competent in addressing the impact of racial trauma and anti-Blackness can help individuals work through generational pain.

- **Support for Community Healing Spaces:** Creating safe spaces for healing within communities allows individuals to process trauma collectively. Black and Indigenous communities benefit from having dedicated centers for community-led support, where individuals can gather for dialogue, workshops, ceremonies, and therapy sessions. Establishing peer support groups, cultural healing events, and educational seminars on mental health awareness can break stigmas surrounding mental health in both communities.

- **Training Healers and Practitioners within the Community:** Investing in training for mental health practitioners from within Black and Indigenous communities helps bridge gaps in cultural understanding. Scholarships, mentorships, and professional support can empower community members to become social workers, therapists, and psychologists, providing culturally resonant care for their own communities.

3. Reparative Justice and Systemic Change

Healing on an individual level is not sufficient without addressing the structural forces that perpetuate dehumanization. Reparative justice involves righting historical wrongs, both through policy changes and by repairing the material harms inflicted on Black and Indigenous communities.

- **Financial Reparations:** Financial reparations for both Black and Indigenous communities are essential to address the economic disparities created by slavery, land theft, and institutional discrimination. For Black Americans, reparations could include direct payments, community investment, student loan forgiveness, and business grants. For Indigenous communities, reparations could involve the restoration of land, financial compensation, and greater tribal sovereignty. Financial reparations acknowledge the material harms inflicted on these communities and allow for economic empowerment.

- **Policy Reforms to End Structural Racism:** Policy reforms in the criminal justice system, healthcare, housing, and education are necessary to dismantle the structures that perpetuate inequality and dehumanization. Ending practices like police brutality, mass incarceration, and discriminatory healthcare policies is essential for healing. Policy reform should also include curriculum changes that provide an accurate representation of American history and the contributions of Black and Indigenous people.

- **Economic Justice Initiatives:** Systemic oppression has resulted in wealth gaps that limit economic opportunities. Initiatives like housing assistance, business grants, and improved access to capital for Black and Indigenous entrepreneurs can empower communities to break cycles of poverty. Supporting cooperative economics and communal wealth-building projects, such as land trusts and mutual aid networks, can enable greater self-sufficiency and economic resilience.

4. Education and Historical Awareness

Education plays a critical role in either perpetuating dehumanizing narratives or fostering healing and truth. Ensuring that all students learn an accurate history of America, including the experiences of Black and Indigenous people, is crucial for dismantling ignorance and fostering empathy.

- **Curriculum Reform:** Reforming school curricula to include comprehensive, accurate accounts of slavery, Indigenous genocide, segregation, and the civil rights struggle is essential. Accurate historical representation not only honors the experiences of Black and Indigenous Americans but also educates all students on the realities of systemic oppression. Programs that promote anti-racist and decolonial education can create more empathetic and informed citizens who are less likely to perpetuate oppressive systems.

- **Supporting Black and Indigenous Teachers:** Representation within education is important. Supporting Black and Indigenous educators who can share culturally relevant perspectives fosters a learning environment where students feel represented and understood. Scholarship programs, professional development, and mentorship initiatives can support Black and Indigenous teachers in creating inclusive classrooms.

- **Community History Projects:** Encouraging students and community members to engage in local history projects allows for the preservation of stories that might otherwise be forgotten. These projects honor the experiences of those who endured dehumanization while empowering younger generations to connect with their heritage. Museums, storytelling programs, and oral history projects can bring community histories to life and provide healing through remembrance.

5. Spiritual and Ancestral Healing

Finally, spiritual and ancestral healing provides a deeply personal and often transformative avenue for healing from dehumanization. Many Black and Indigenous people find strength in reclaiming spiritual practices that were either demonized or taken from them.

- **Reconnection with Ancestral Practices:** For both Black and Indigenous Americans, connecting with spiritual practices—whether through prayer, meditation, or ceremony—can provide grounding and continuity. These practices serve as a reminder of resilience and survival across generations. Encouraging the exploration of African, Caribbean, and Indigenous spiritual practices, which often center on community, nature, and interdependence, allows individuals to heal through reconnection.

- **Intergenerational Healing:** Intergenerational trauma requires intergenerational solutions. Programs that facilitate conversations between elders and youth allow for the transmission of cultural knowledge, resilience strategies, and ancestral pride. These exchanges can break cycles of trauma and empower younger generations to navigate modern challenges while grounded in cultural identity.

- **Forging Alliances and Solidarity:** For both communities, solidarity with other marginalized groups can foster a sense of shared purpose and collective healing. Forging alliances with others working toward equity and justice provides a broader support network and reduces isolation.

Healing from the dehumanizing legacy of systemic oppression is a journey that requires acknowledgment, reclamation, and transformation. For Black and Indigenous Americans, healing solutions must address the historical and ongoing harms caused by dehumanization while empowering individuals to reclaim their sense of humanity, dignity, and agency. Through cultural revival, mental health support, reparative justice, educational reform, and spiritual healing, Black and Indigenous communities can build pathways to resilience and renewal. The work of healing is a collective endeavor, one that demands the dismantling of oppressive systems, the honoring of ancestral wisdom, and the creation of spaces where all people can thrive.

CHAPTER 9

Restorative Justice as a Pathway to Healing:

Addressing the Legacy of Injustice

In the United States and around the world, marginalized communities continue to grapple with the enduring consequences of historical injustices. From slavery and segregation to colonialism and systemic discrimination, these acts have caused deep harm that persists across generations. Restorative justice, with its emphasis on repairing harm and fostering healing, provides an essential framework for addressing these injustices. Unlike traditional justice, which focuses on punishment, restorative justice centers on accountability, healing, and reconciliation. This chapter explores the critical importance of restorative justice, offering approaches to restitution, reparations, and memorialization, and examining how education, commemoration, and inclusivity can foster a collective healing process.

Understanding Restorative Justice in the Context of Historical Injustices

Restorative justice is a philosophy that seeks to restore balance by addressing harm through reparative measures rather than punitive actions. It encourages accountability, truth-telling, and efforts to repair relationships and restore dignity to those who have been wronged. When applied to historical injustices, restorative justice goes beyond individual acts and aims to address systemic harms, such as slavery, indigenous dispossession, racial discrimination, and other forms of structural inequality.

The goals of restorative justice in this context are:

- Acknowledge past injustices openly and honestly.
- Hold accountable those who perpetuated harm, either directly or indirectly.
- Repair harm through tangible actions, such as financial reparations, community investment, and policy changes.
- Create conditions for ongoing reconciliation, healing, and understanding between affected communities and society at large.

By addressing historical wrongs, restorative justice helps restore the dignity of marginalized communities, fosters trust in institutions, and works toward a more equitable society.

Approaches to Restitution, Reparations, and Memorialization

To operationalize restorative justice, various strategies are needed to ensure that past wrongs are acknowledged and addressed in meaningful ways. These strategies include restitution, reparations, and memorialization.

Restitution

Restitution involves providing compensation for tangible losses experienced by marginalized communities. In the context of historical injustices, restitution can take various forms:

- Land Reclamation for Indigenous Communities: Restitution may involve returning lands to Indigenous tribes and communities. This is a tangible means of addressing the loss of ancestral lands, as well as the cultural and spiritual connections disrupted by colonialism. Land restitution empowers Indigenous communities to regain control over their territories, restoring autonomy and cultural continuity.
- Legal Reforms and Policy Changes: Legal restitution is often necessary to amend discriminatory policies that continue to harm marginalized communities. By repealing unjust laws, revising educational curricula, and implementing policies that promote equality, society acknowledges past harm and works toward structural change.

Reparations

Reparations go beyond restitution by addressing the broader impact of systemic harm. Reparations acknowledge that past injustices have created intergenerational trauma and economic disparities, which require sustained investments to repair.

- Financial Reparations: Financial compensation can address the economic harms inflicted by slavery, segregation, and land dispossession. Direct payments to descendants of enslaved people or financial compensation to Indigenous communities serve as both a material acknowledgment of harm and a step toward economic justice.
- Community Investments: Reparations may also involve investments in education, healthcare, housing, and business development in historically marginalized communities. Funding initiatives, scholarships, and healthcare programs that benefit Black and Indigenous populations can help close gaps created by centuries of systemic oppression. Community reparations are particularly valuable as they support communal healing and resilience-building.

- Educational and Institutional Reforms: Reparations may include the restructuring of institutions, such as universities, that have benefited from past injustices. This might involve creating scholarships for descendants of marginalized groups, renaming buildings, or investing in educational programs that explore the true history of these institutions and their complicity in oppression.

Memorialization

Memorialization is the process of commemorating past injustices and honoring the resilience of marginalized communities. It is a vital aspect of restorative justice as it acknowledges the experiences of those who suffered and ensures that future generations understand the full scope of history.

- Monuments and Memorials: Erecting monuments, museums, and memorials dedicated to historical injustices is a way to visibly honor the memory of those who suffered. Such spaces serve as a reminder of the past and provide a location for reflection, education, and mourning. Examples include the National Memorial for Peace and Justice in Alabama, which commemorates victims of lynching, and the United States Holocaust Memorial Museum, which educates the public about the atrocities of the Holocaust.
- Public Commemorations and Remembrance Days: Establishing national or local days of remembrance can promote awareness and collective mourning. Events that commemorate the lives lost to slavery, genocide, or violence allow communities to come together and reflect on shared history. This practice of remembrance reinforces society's commitment to justice and honors the resilience of survivors and their descendants.
- Storytelling and Oral Histories: Collecting and sharing the stories of individuals who experienced injustice is essential for preserving cultural memory. Oral history projects that record and amplify the voices of Black, Indigenous, and other marginalized individuals give dignity to their lived experiences and educate future generations. This is especially powerful for communities whose histories have been erased or misrepresented.

The Importance of Education, Commemoration, and Promoting Inclusivity

Restorative justice requires a societal shift in how we understand and engage with history. Education, commemoration, and inclusivity are essential components in this process, helping to foster empathy, awareness, and a commitment to equity.

Education

Education is the foundation of restorative justice because it provides the knowledge and context needed to understand historical injustices. Acknowledging the full scope of history is essential for addressing past harms.

- Curriculum Reform: Incorporating accurate and comprehensive history into school curricula helps students understand the roots of systemic inequality and the importance of justice. By learning about the realities of slavery, segregation, and Indigenous displacement, students are encouraged to think critically about societal issues and develop empathy for those affected.
- Anti-Racist and Decolonial Education: Integrating anti-racist and decolonial perspectives into education can help dismantle biases and promote inclusivity. Programs that explore the history and contributions of Black and Indigenous people foster a more balanced and just understanding of American history.

Commemoration

Commemoration provides an opportunity for individuals and communities to reflect on historical injustices collectively. Through memorials, events, and storytelling, commemoration keeps the memory of injustice alive, encouraging society to honor victims and commit to progress.

- Annual Events and Observances: Events such as Martin Luther King Jr. Day, Indigenous Peoples' Day, and Juneteenth remind society of the importance of justice, equality, and reconciliation. Observing these days promotes collective recognition of past wrongs and reinforces commitments to justice and equity.
- Intergenerational Dialogue: Facilitating conversations between older and younger generations allows the transmission of knowledge, resilience, and healing strategies. Such dialogue can foster understanding, create bonds, and ensure that the memory of past struggles is not lost.

Promoting Inclusivity

Inclusivity is crucial to ensuring that all voices are heard and respected within society. An inclusive approach to restorative justice not only addresses harm but also values and uplifts marginalized perspectives.

- Diverse Representation: Representation of Black, Indigenous, and other marginalized groups within leadership positions, media, and education helps to normalize inclusivity and challenge stereotypes. Representation fosters belonging and affirms the humanity of all individuals, counteracting the dehumanization that has historically impacted marginalized communities.
- Community-Led Solutions: Centering the voices of Black and Indigenous communities in the development and implementation of restorative justice initiatives empowers those directly affected by historical injus-

tices. Community-led solutions are likely to be more effective, as they are grounded in lived experience and local knowledge.

- Building Solidarity: Promoting inclusivity also involves building alliances across racial, ethnic, and socioeconomic lines. Solidarity among communities facing oppression can amplify efforts for justice and create a collective commitment to human rights and equality.

The journey toward healing from historical injustices requires collective effort, understanding, and a commitment to restorative justice. Through restitution, reparations, memorialization, and a dedication to education, commemoration, and inclusivity, our society can begin to repair the harm inflicted on marginalized communities. Healing is an ongoing process, but by addressing the root causes of injustice and fostering a culture of respect, empathy, and accountability, a more just and humane American society can be built. This work not only restores dignity to those who have suffered but also strengthens the social fabric, ensuring that future generations inherit a legacy of justice rather than oppression.

CHAPTER 10
Building a Just and Equitable Society for All

A truly just and equitable society is one in which all individuals, regardless of their race, gender, socioeconomic status, or background, have equal access to opportunities, resources, and the ability to live lives free of discrimination and oppression. However, in the United States and around the world, systemic racism and inequality continue to create barriers for marginalized communities, especially Black and Indigenous people and other people of color. Achieving a just and equitable society is not only a moral imperative, but it is also essential for the health, stability, and prosperity of nations. In this chapter, we explore the importance of building a society rooted in justice and equity, examine strategies for dismantling systemic racism and promoting social justice, and discuss the roles that individuals, communities, and institutions play in creating lasting, transformative change.

The Importance of Building a Just and Equitable Society

A just and equitable society benefits everyone, creating environments in which all people have the opportunity to reach their full potential.

When justice and equity are prioritized, societies become more stable, innovative, and resilient. In contrast, systemic inequality undermines social cohesion, fosters resentment, and leads to harmful disparities in areas such as health, education, employment, and housing.

- Economic Stability and Growth: Inequality and discrimination are not only moral failings but also have economic consequences. Research shows that reducing racial and gender inequality can boost economic productivity, as marginalized communities gain access to education and employment opportunities that enable them to contribute more effectively to the economy.

- Health and Well-being: Systemic racism and inequality create significant health disparities. For example, Black and Indigenous communities often experience higher rates of chronic illness and lower life expectancy due to limited access to healthcare, economic stress, and exposure to environmental toxins. Building a just and equitable society can reduce these health disparities and improve quality of life for all.

- Social Cohesion: Injustices and disparities fuel social unrest and division. By building a society that values justice and equity, communities become stronger, more cohesive, and better equipped to handle crises. A fair and inclusive society cultivates empathy, trust, and mutual support, creating a foundation for long-term stability.

To build a just society, we must address the structural barriers that prevent marginalized communities from accessing equal opportunities. This requires a commitment to systemic change at every level of society, as well as active participation from individuals, communities, and institutions.

Strategies for Dismantling Systemic Racism and Promoting Social Justice

Systemic racism is embedded within the policies, institutions, and practices that shape daily life. Therefore, dismantling systemic racism requires both structural and cultural shifts that address the root causes of inequality. Strategies for promoting social justice must be comprehensive, sustained, and intentional.

Policy Reform and Legislative Change

One of the most effective ways to dismantle systemic racism is through policy reform. Government policies have historically perpetuated inequality through practices such as redlining, voter suppression, and discriminatory criminal justice policies. Reforming these policies and passing new legislation that promotes equity is essential for creating lasting change.

- Criminal Justice Reform: The criminal justice system has disproportionately targeted Black, Indigenous, and other communities of color, resulting in mass incarceration, police violence, and over-policing in marginalized neighborhoods. Policies such as ending cash bail, reforming sentencing laws, decriminalizing non-violent offenses, and investing in community-based alternatives to incarceration can reduce racial disparities in the justice system.

- Educational Equity: Access to quality education is essential for social mobility, but racial disparities in education funding, resources, and access to advanced courses continue to limit opportunities for students of color. Advocating for equitable school funding, diverse curricula, and policies that reduce segregation can help create a fairer education system that benefits all students.

- Healthcare Access and Environmental Justice: Health disparities disproportionately affect marginalized communities, particularly in relation to access to healthcare, safe housing, and clean environments. Policies that expand healthcare access, address food deserts, and ensure environmental protections in marginalized communities are essential for achieving health equity.

Economic Justice and Wealth Redistribution

Economic inequality is deeply intertwined with racial inequality, as systemic racism has excluded marginalized communities from wealth-building opportunities for generations. Addressing economic disparities is essential for creating a society in which all individuals have the resources needed to thrive.

- Reparations and Restitution: Reparations for slavery, Indigenous land dispossession, and other forms of historical injustice are essential for addressing the generational impact of systemic racism. Reparations can take the form of direct financial payments, investments in communities, and policies aimed at reducing wealth inequality.

- Living Wages and Workers' Rights: Low-wage workers, particularly people of color, often face exploitative working conditions, inadequate pay, and lack of benefits. Ensuring a living wage, protecting workers' rights to organize, and supporting fair labor practices help uplift marginalized communities and reduce economic disparities.

- Affordable Housing: Housing discrimination and gentrification have forced many marginalized communities into impoverished, under-resourced neighborhoods. Investing in affordable housing, preventing displacement, and creating pathways to homeownership for historically excluded communities can promote economic stability and wealth-building opportunities.

Educational and Cultural Change

Systemic racism is not only structural but also cultural, as biases and stereotypes shape perceptions, policies, and social norms. Education and cultural shifts are vital for promoting social justice and creating a society that values diversity, equity, and inclusion.

- Anti-Racism Education and Training: Schools, workplaces, and institutions should incorporate anti-racism education to address biases and foster empathy. Programs that teach the history of racism and the importance of social justice can help individuals recognize their own biases and challenge discriminatory attitudes.

- Diverse Representation and Inclusion: Increasing representation of marginalized groups in media, politics, and leadership positions can shift societal perceptions and promote inclusivity. When people see themselves represented in influential spaces, it challenges stereotypes, empowers communities, and fosters a sense of belonging.

- Public Commemoration and Memorialization: Acknowledging the history of racial violence and oppression through memorials, museums, and public events is essential for reconciliation. Memorializing the struggles and achievements of marginalized communities promotes healing, honors resilience, and keeps history from being forgotten.

The Role of Individuals, Communities, and Institutions in Creating Lasting Change

Creating a just and equitable society is a shared responsibility that requires the active participation of individuals, communities, and institutions. Each group has a unique role to play in promoting social justice, challenging racism, and dismantling oppressive systems.

The Role of Individuals

Individuals have the power to effect change through their actions, choices, and advocacy. By educating themselves, challenging biases, and using their voices, individuals can contribute to a culture that values justice and equity.

- Education and Self-Reflection: Learning about systemic racism, privilege, and inequality is the first step toward creating change. Individuals should be willing to reflect on their own biases, challenge stereotypes, and recognize how their actions impact marginalized communities.

- Allyship and Advocacy: Being an ally means standing in solidarity with marginalized communities, amplifying their voices, and advocating for policies that promote justice. Allies can use their privilege to support social justice movements, challenge discrimination, and push for systemic change.

- Community Engagement: Individuals can make a difference within their communities by participating in local initiatives, volunteering, and supporting organizations that promote equity. Grassroots efforts at the community level often lead to lasting, positive change.

The Role of Communities

Communities play an essential role in supporting marginalized individuals, creating safe spaces for healing, and fostering unity. Communities that work together toward a common vision of equity and justice can create transformative change.

- Community-Based Organizations and Advocacy Groups: Many organizations work directly within communities to address issues such as housing, education, healthcare, and criminal justice. These organizations provide resources, empower individuals, and advocate for policies that promote equity.

- Collective Action: Collective action within communities can drive change, as demonstrated by movements such as Black Lives Matter and environmental justice campaigns. When communities come together to demand justice, they can bring attention to systemic issues and pressure institutions to act.

- Healing and Resilience Building: Marginalized communities have endured trauma and oppression for generations, making healing and resilience-building essential. Programs that promote mental health, cultural pride, and community support help foster healing and create stronger, more empowered communities.

The Role of Institutions

Institutions—including government, corporations, schools, and religious organizations—hold significant power and responsibility for creating an equitable society. Institutional commitment to diversity, equity, and inclusion is essential for addressing systemic racism.

- Government Accountability and Policy Change: Government institutions have the power to create and enforce laws that protect civil rights, reduce disparities, and promote equality. Holding government accountable through voting, advocacy, and public pressure is essential for achieving justice.

- Corporate Responsibility and Diversity Initiatives: Corporations can promote social justice by addressing discrimination within the workplace, implementing diversity and inclusion initiatives, and supporting policies that promote equity. Corporate social responsibility extends beyond profit to include ethical practices that benefit society.

- Educational Institutions and Curricular Reform: Schools and universities shape societal beliefs and values. By incorporating anti-racism education, promoting diversity in curricula, and supporting equitable practices, educational institutions can help dismantle systemic racism and foster social justice.

Building a just and equitable society is a complex but essential endeavor that requires commitment from individuals, communities, and institutions alike. Dismantling systemic racism and promoting social justice are not tasks that can be achieved overnight, nor can they be addressed solely through isolated efforts. Instead, creating lasting change demands a sustained, collective effort that addresses the structural, cultural, and personal dimensions of inequality.

The journey toward justice requires empathy, education, and action. By recognizing the importance of equity, implementing strategies for systemic reform, and acknowledging our shared humanity, we can work together to create a society that offers dignity, respect, and opportunity for all. The pursuit of justice and equity is not merely a goal but a continuous process—one that calls us to remain vigilant, hopeful, and committed to building a better future.

CONCLUSION
Our Journey Towards Healing and Unity

In our journey towards healing and unity, we have delved deep into the dehumanizing history and its lasting impacts on America. From the displacement of the Indigenous people (Native Americans); to the brutal enslavement of Africans to the systemic oppression faced by Black Americans, the dehumanization that permeated every aspect of society has left a profound mark on our collective consciousness. We have explored the Civil Rights movement, the struggles for justice, and the heroic figures who fought for equality, only to be met with violence and tragedy.

Throughout this book, we have examined the dehumanizing mindset of slave owners, the intentional portrayal of White and Black people in the media, the systemic injustices embedded in laws and institutions, and the ongoing trauma and post-traumatic slave syndrome that continue to afflict communities today. It is evident that the wounds run deep, and the road to healing is long.

But there is hope. We have looked to the lessons of history, drawing inspiration from the Truth and Reconciliation Commission in South

Africa and the healing journey undertaken by Germany after the Holocaust. These examples demonstrate that it is possible to confront the past, acknowledge the atrocities committed, and work towards reconciliation and unity.

To heal our nation, we must confront the uncomfortable truths of our history, educate ourselves and future generations about the depths of dehumanization, and actively dismantle the systems of oppression that perpetuate inequality. Healing requires the engagement of individuals, communities, and institutions, all working in unison towards a common goal of justice and equity.

Restorative justice must play a central role in this process. It demands that we acknowledge the pain and suffering inflicted upon generations of Native and Black Americans and take concrete steps to repair the harm done. It calls for restitution, reparations, and the creation of spaces for dialogue, understanding, and healing. We must ensure that the stories of those who were dehumanized are preserved and shared, so that we never forget the injustices committed and the resilience of those who endured them.

But healing goes beyond material reparations and legal frameworks. It requires a fundamental shift in our collective mindset—a reimagining of our society as one that values the inherent worth and dignity of every individual, regardless of their race, ethnicity, or background. It calls for empathy, compassion, and a commitment to unlearning the biases and stereotypes that have perpetuated division.

As we conclude this book, let us remember that the journey towards healing and unity is not easy, but it is necessary. We must summon the courage to confront our past, embrace uncomfortable conversations, and work towards dismantling the structures that uphold dehumanization. It is through collective action, guided by principles of justice, equality, and love, that we can forge a future where every person is seen, heard, and valued.

May this book serve as a catalyst for introspection, dialogue, and transformative change. Let us embark on this journey together, hand in hand, with a shared commitment to healing, unity, and a more just and equitable society for all.

In the words of Dr. Martin Luther King Jr., "We may have all come on different ships, but we're in the same boat now." It is time to chart a new course, where the wounds of dehumanization are healed, and the promise of liberty and justice becomes a living reality for every American.

Together, we can build a future that not only acknowledges the past but also creates a society where the dehumanization of any human being is unthinkable. Let us take this transformative journey towards healing and unity, paving the way for a brighter and more inclusive future for generations to come. Ultimately living up to and forever aspiring to be One Nation, Under God, Indivisible, with Liberty and Justice for ALL.

REFERENCES

Books and Academic Texts

Alexander, M. (2012). The New Jim Crow: Mass Incarceration in the Age of Colorblindness. The New Press.

Anderson, C. (2017). White Rage: The Unspoken Truth of Our Racial Divide. Bloomsbury USA.

Baptist, E. E. (2014). The Half Has Never Been Told: Slavery and the Making of American Capitalism. Basic Books.

Berlin, I. (2003). Generations of Captivity: A History of African-American Slaves. Belknap Press.

Coates, T.-N. (2015). Between the World and Me. Spiegel & Grau.

DeGruy, J. (2005). Post Traumatic Slave Syndrome: America's Legacy of Enduring Injury and Healing. Joy DeGruy Publications.

Du Bois, W. E. B. (1935). Black Reconstruction in America: 1860-1880. The Free Press.

Feagin, J. (2013). The White Racial Frame: Centuries of Racial Framing and Counter-Framing. Routledge.

Kendi, I. X. (2019). How to Be an Antiracist. One World.

King, M. L., Jr. (1967). Where Do We Go from Here: Chaos or Community? Beacon Press.

Morrison, T. (1992). Playing in the Dark: Whiteness and the Literary Imagination. Vintage Books.

Wilkerson, I. (2020). Caste: The Origins of Our Discontents. Random House.

Woodson, C. G. (1933). The Mis-Education of the Negro. Associated Publishers.

Historical and Government Documents

United States Constitution, 13th Amendment (1865).

Douglass, F. (1852). What to the Slave is the Fourth of July? Speech.

"Black Codes" of Southern States (1865-1866).

Brown v. Board of Education, 347 U.S. 483 (1954).

Civil Rights Act of 1964, Pub. L. No. 88-352, 78 Stat. 241.

Journal Articles and Reports

Bowser, B. P. (2017). "Racism: Origin and Theory," Journal of Black Studies, 48(6), 572-590.

Butler, P. (2017). "The System Is Working the Way It Is Supposed To: The Limits of Criminal Justice Reform," Georgetown Law Journal, 104, 1419-1479.

Green, E. R. (2020). "The Lingering Effects of Slavery on Black Economic Inequality in the United States," Economic History Review, 73(2), 439-462.

Krieger, N. (2020). "Discrimination and Health Inequities: A Critical Review of the Evidence," Annual Review of Public Health, 41, 245-264.

Roberts, D. E. (1997). "The Welfare Debate and the Social Construction of Black Citizenship," Yale Law Journal, 108(8), 2573-2583.

Stevenson, B. (2015). Just Mercy: A Story of Justice and Redemption. Spiegel & Grau.

Articles and Websites

Equal Justice Initiative. (n.d.). "Lynching in America: Confronting the Legacy of Racial Terror." Retrieved from https://eji.org/reports/lynching-in-america/

National Museum of African American History and Culture. (n.d.). "Slavery and Freedom." Retrieved from https://nmaahc.si.edu/

National Public Radio (NPR). (2020). "The Racial Reckoning in America: Exploring America's Past of Racial Injustice." Retrieved from https://www.npr.org/

Southern Poverty Law Center (SPLC). (n.d.). "Teaching Hard History: American Slavery." Retrieved from https://www.splcenter.org/

Media and Documentaries

Ava DuVernay (Director). (2016). 13th [Film]. Netflix.

Peck, R. (Director). (2017). I Am Not Your Negro. Magnolia Pictures.

Raoul Peck (Director). (2021). Exterminate All the Brutes [TV Series]. HBO.

Shenk, S. & Davidson, R. (Directors). (2006). The Rape of Recy Taylor [Film]. August Films.

"Eyes on the Prize" (1987). [Documentary Series]. PBS.

Psychology and Sociology Studies

Fanon, F. (1961). The Wretched of the Earth. Grove Press.

Hartman, S. V. (2007). Lose Your Mother: A Journey Along the Atlantic Slave Route. Farrar, Straus and Giroux.

hooks, bell. (1992). Black Looks: Race and Representation. South End Press.

Jones, J. (1981). Bad Blood: The Tuskegee Syphilis Experiment. The Free Press.

Smedley, A. (1993). Race in North America: Origin and Evolution of a Worldview. Westview Press.

Smith, L. T. (1999). Decolonizing Methodologies: Research and Indigenous Peoples. Zed Books.

Additional Sources on Healing and Reconciliation

Akbar, N. (1984). Chains and Images of Psychological Slavery. Mind Productions & Associates.

DeGruy, J. (2005). Post Traumatic Slave Syndrome: America's Legacy of Enduring Injury and Healing. Joy DeGruy Publications.

Tutu, D. (1999). No Future Without Forgiveness. Image.

Wilderson III, F. B. (2020). Afropessimism. Liveright.

Indigenous Rights and History

Dunbar-Ortiz, R. (2014). An Indigenous Peoples' History of the United States. Beacon Press.

Smith, A. (2005). Conquest: Sexual Violence and American Indian Genocide. South End Press.

Warrior, R. (1995). Tribal Secrets: Recovering American Indian Intellectual Traditions. University of Minnesota Press.